PLAYS BY LYNNE ALVAREZ: LATER PLAYS AND SELECTED POEMS

BROADWAY PLAY PUBLISHING INC
224 E 62nd St, NY, NY 10065
www.broadwayplaypub.com
info@broadwayplaypub.com

PLAYS BY LYNNE ALVAREZ: LATER PLAYS AND POETRY
© Copyright 2008 by Lynne Alvarez

All rights reserved. This work is fully protected under the copyright laws of the United States of America.

No part of this publication may be photocopied, reproduced, stored in a retrieval system, or transmitted, in any form or by any means, electronic, mechanical, recording, or otherwise, without the prior permission of the publisher. Additional copies of this play are available from the publisher.

Written permission is required for live performance of any sort. This includes readings, cuttings, scenes, and excerpts. For amateur and stock performances of ROMOLA AND NIJINSKY, please contact Broadway Play Publishing Inc. For all other rights contact The Susan Gurman Agency, 14 Penn Plaza, Suite 1703, NY NY 10122, 212 749-4618.

Cover photo by Katherine Owens

First printing: August 2008
This printing: July 2016
I S B N: 978-0-88145-394-2

Book design: Marie Donovan
Word processing: Microsoft Word
Typographic controls: Ventura Publisher
Typeface: Palatino
Printed and bound in the U S A

CONTENTS

About the Author v
Mac Wellman: Apropos of Lynne Alvarez vi
ESPERANZA RISING 1
ROMOLA AND NIJINSKY 57
THE SNOW QUEEN 103
Selected poems 151
Part I: Poems from Nautla 155
Part II: Ceremonies of the Earth 183

ABOUT THE AUTHOR

Lynne Alvarez arrived in New York in 1977 planning to be a hot shot poet and die young. In the first matter—she won a CAPS grant for poetry in 1979 and served on the Poets & Writers board of directors for ten years—as Vice President of the board for four years. She did succeed in publishing much poetry, giving many readings and had two books of poetry published by Waterfront Press—*the dreaming man* (1981) and *living with numbers* (1986)—and became a member of PEN. But in the second matter she continued to live and her attention turned abruptly to playwriting in 1978.

On a whim, Alvarez accompanied a friend to a gathering of Hispanic writers at Miriam Colon's Puerto Rican Traveling Theater. At thirty-one she had never thought of writing a play, but she was now hooked. She wrote two plays under the auspices of this workshop—GRACIELA, which was presented by the Puerto Rican Traveling Theater and THE GUITARRON, which premiered at the Saint Clements Theater in 1984 and won her an N E A fellowship and entry into New Dramatists. It was first published in 1985 in T C G's anthology, *On New Ground*. She was a member of New Dramatists for seven years (1979-1987) and continues to be a proud alumna of the same. There she wrote several plays including HIDDEN PARTS (1981) which won a Kesselring Award in 1983 and premiered at Primary Stages later that year; THE WONDERFUL TOWER OF HUMBERT LAVOIGNET, which won two awards—The Le Compte de Nouey Award in 1984 and an F D G/C B S Award for Best Play and later Best Production at Capital Repertory Theater in Albany, NY in 1984/85, and was published by Broadway Play Publishing Inc. In 1984, The Actor's Theater of Louisville commissioned a one-act play which became THIN AIR: TALES FROM A REVOLUTION. THIN AIR premiered at San Diego Repertory Theater in 1987 and won a Drama League Award and a Rockefeller Fellowship in 1988.

Two New York Foundation grants followed in 1994 and 1998, years in which she also wrote three plays for San Francisco's ACT Conservatory—THE REINCARNATION OF JAIMIE BROWN, EDDIE/MUNDO/EDMUNDO and ANALIESE. All three were premiered there and were published variously in the Smith & Kraus anthologies *Best plays by Women 1994* and *Best Plays by Women 1997, Best Plays for Young Audiences* etc. Lincoln Center Institute commissioned Alvarez to adapt AND NOW MIGUEL (produced in its 1995 season). The Repertory of St. Louis also commissioned two children's plays, which they produced in 1991 and

1992—RATS, a musical based on the Pied Piper of Hamlin, and RIKKI TIKKI TAVI. Smith & Kraus published her *Collected Plays, Volume* I in 2000.

Alvarez has been commissioned as a translator of plays and poetry as well. In 1988, she translated Fernando Arrabal's new play THE DAMSEL AND THE GORILLA OR THE RED MADONNA for INTAR's production. In 1990 she translated and adapted Tirso de Molina's DON JUAN OF SEVILLE for Classic Stage Company's New York production and most recently has translated three plays of the Mexican playwright, Felipe Santander. These were published as a collection by Smith & Kraus in 2002 and were subsidized for a three-year period (1999-2002) by grants from The Peter Sharp Foundation and The Evelyn Sharp Foundation. Alvarez also received a two-year grant (2000-2002) from the Guggenheim Museum's Works & Process program to write DEUX MARIAGES: ROMOLA AND NIJINSKY that premiered at Primary Stages in New York in May 2003 and has been published in Smith & Kraus's anthology Best Plays by Women 2001 and as an individual play by Broadway Play Publishing Inc in 2004.

APROPOS OF LYNNE ALVAREZ
Mac Wellman

This is an important book: Alvarez has been writing plays and poetry of a very high order for several decades now. She is known to a few, but not by as many, in my view, as is warranted by the very special qualities of the work. Looking at her latest plays, ROMOLA AND NIJINSKY and THE SNOW QUEEN, I am struck by how her standards have remained; indeed, the latter strike me as the strongest in her oeuvre—a remarkable and beautiful play about love and loss (and so much else). She may be our only true Symbolist playwright, in the vein of Strindberg, Maeterlinck, Blok and Yeats.

~

The sea roars and swells
above me
my lone heart leaps
that dolphin part of me.

~

And yet.

Symbolism is a theater of the mind, an interior theater that acts out a deadly serious rebellion against the Bourgeois world of appearances, and the theater of that world—naturalism and the more unthinking and knee-jerk varieties of realism. What most people (who do not much care for theater unless they are being tourists in New York or subscribers at the better class of regional theater) think of as *theater* on those rare occasions when they think of it at all. The symbolists denied the realism so heartedly embraced by their social betters, and regarded this world much as the Gnostics and Neoplatonists did, as a putrid hell ruled by a malevolent lesser demon, or demiurge. Ironically, one the inventors of naturalism, Strindberg was also one of the inventors of symbolism.

But Alvarez's theater is something altogether different, it is complex without being nihilistic. It is both for and against the world, it is true, but the mood is far more light-hearted and sophisticated.

~

He said all women are whores
and to prove it he sent

his mother postcards and fruit
and whispered phone calls
until she agreed to meet with him.
And when she walked through the door
pale and anxious in black
her heart full of colors
he flashed his teeth and said
"You see, all women are whores".

~

This is a tricky kind of theater, easy to make a mess of, and often possessed of an unmoored quality that drives the typical contemporary audience to distraction. But Alvarez has a very clear sense of how far she can go with her visionary and hallucinatory drama; and hence the stories she tells are always clear and sharp, frequently witty, and silly (in the best sense) and never portentous and pretentious as so much "poetical" theater is. ROMOLA AND NIJINSKY and THE SNOW QUEEN are about the theatrics and folly of love without being *against* love. These are sad, wise plays that do not feel particular sad and wise. Hence THE SNOW QUEEN feels as much like Hans Christian Andersen as the morose Strindberg. And the wonderful images of birds, birds, birds- toucans, peacocks, swans, geese, seagull, storks, falcons and vultures appear, enact their own special kind of theater and are gone. Their world overlaid on ours, very, or is it just the reverse? They symbolize something, but it is hard to pinpoint just exactly what.

~

The ball stopped in mid air,
white against a sky,
undiluted,
so blue your eyes tear
with the immensity of its
precision.

~

And yet. And yet.

She is an Argentine-American, and spent nine years in south of the border where she was a journalist in Mexico City. People pointed guns at her. (I suspect she carried her own!) Her ESPERANZA RISING is a striking piece of political theater that depicts the dizzying world of Mexicans displaced during the Depression by class strife at home, and left to fend for themselves in a pitiless and reactionary North America. (In part the play is an adaptation of Muñoz Ryan's book by the same name.) The title character herself is as tempest tossed as the fascinating outsider artist Martin Ramirez, whose strange and wonderful work recently was shown at the Folk Arts Museum here in New York. Indeed, you can feel the inexorable lines of force that run through this haunting play as much as you can see them in Ramirez's paintings.

Her precision (also in her fine poetry quoted above) is striking and passionate and always assured. In her clarity, she is about as readable as any playwright I know. Would that more were working in this very special vein, but we are most fortunate to have her.

Recently I saw a wonderful painting by another woman whose work is not well enough known, Ree Morton. In the painting are words nestled on a wonderful scroll:

"The responsibility of the artist
...to be free & while in that
freedom, to look, and to see
while looking, and to feel, and
to respond while feeling, and to
romantic, and to love the
romance."

My friend Lynne Alvarez could have written that.

A NOTE FROM THE PUBLISHER
Christopher Gould

Thirty years ago I came to New York, a year after Lynne. One of the first things I did was to start reading plays for the then new Women's Project. One of the first plays I read was Lynne's THE GUITARRÓN. What a lovely, poetic and beautiful play it is. Lynne captured a special place in my heart then, and a few years after I started publishing plays, I was thrilled to start a relationship with her with THE WONDERFUL TOWER OF HUMBERT LAVOIGNET. It is a joy and honor to continue that with this book.

Christopher Gould

ESPERANZA RISING

*adapted from the book by
Pam Muñoz Ryan*

The world premiere was at Children's Theater Company, Minneapolis, MN, from 14 March-15 April 2006. The cast and creative contributors were:

ESPERANZA	Erin Nicole Hampe
HORTENSIA	Catalina Maynard
DON SIXTO/ALFONSO	Raul Ramos
MIGUEL	Desmin Borges
LUIS	Bob Davis
SERVANT GIRL/ISABEL	Maeve Moynihan
MARIELENA	Celeste J Busa
MARTA	Amanda Granger
OKIE FATHER	Leif Jurgenson
OKIE MOTHER	Rebecca Lord
OKIE BOY	Albert Dudek
ENSEMBLE	Chelsea Bohmer, Tegan Carr, Jacob Duhon, Patrick Faunillan, Kate Howell, Ryan Howell, Katie Moss, Natasha Roy, Gabrielle Silverman, Kaliya Warren

Vihuela & guitar	Roberto Rodriguez
Guitarron & guitar	Joe Cruz
Accordion & guitar	Victor Zupanc
Director	Rebecca Lynn Brown
Music composition & sound design	Victor Zupanc
Scenic design	Riccardo Hernandez
Costume design	James Schuette
Lighting design	Matt Frey
Dramaturg	Elissa Adams
Choreography	Joe Chvala
Stage manager	Chris Schweiger
Assistant stage manager	Jody Gavin
Stage management apprentice	Megan Traina

CHARACTERS & SETTING

ESPERANZA, *wealthy rancher's daughter*
HORTENSIA, *maid from Oaxaca*
THREE MARIACHIS, *musicians/clowns/mailman*
DON SIXTO, *landowner,* ESPERANZA's *father*
RAMONA, ESPERANZA's *mother,* SIXTO's *wife*
SERVANT GIRL, *eight years old*
MARIELENA, ESPERANZA's *best friend*
MIGUEL, *ranch hand,* HORTENSIA's *son*
LUIS, SIXTO's *brother, town mayor, bank owner*
"Okie" family:
BOY, *eight years old*
FATHER
MOTHER
ISABEL, *eight years old,* MIGUEL's *cousin*
MODESTA, ISABEL's *young mother,* HORTENSIA's *sister-in-law*
ALFONSO, MODESTA's *husband,* HORTENSIA's *brother*
MARTA, MODESTA's *sister*

WOMEN, WORKERS I,II *and* III

There are also crowd scenes with peasant workers, people crossing the border, neighbors at the camp, guards, strikers, workers at the fiesta. All actors not in a specific scene can be used as part of the crowd in that scene.

All action takes place between 1929-1930 at Rancho Linda Flor, at the Mexico-U S A border crossing and at various locations at the workers camp in California.

ACT ONE

Scene One

(Opening song:)

MARIACHI 1: *(Shouts over music)* Mexico!

MARIACHI 2: *Viva Mexico!*

MARIACHI 3: *Viva Mexico!*

ALL: *Bonito es Mexico entero*
Bella tierra nacional
Donde Dios puso un letrero
Como esta no hay otra igual!

MARIACHI 1: Yes. Yes. I love you Mexico!

MARIACHI 2: *Mexico Lindo!*

MARIACHI 3: *Ahora en ingles!*

ALL: All of Mexico is beautiful
As seen with loving eyes
Where God himself put up a sign
This is paradise!

MARIACHI 1: You tell them!

MARIACHI 2: Okay!

ALL: *La Virgen tendio su manto*
En la tierra de amor
Y con eso hizo el rancho
Que se llama linda flor!

MARIACHI 3: Yes. Yes. El Rancho Linda Flor

MARIACHI 1: In the state of Aguascalientes!

ALL: The Virgen spread her mantle
Over a land that she adored
And so created *el rancho*
That we now call Linda Flor.

(The stage is dark except for a splendid bed looking as if it is suspended in air. Among the white lace covers and many ruffled and beaded white pillows we see

movement. ESPERANZA *turns over in her sleep, dressed in a white silk and lace nightgown. At first looks like part of the bed, but we see her dark head move. She lifts her head and suddenly a huge pile of colorfully wrapped birthday presents lights up at the foot of her bed. She sits up and as she does* HORTENSIA *in local dress rushes in carrying a silver tray with a brush and roses on it.*)

HORTENSIA: They're coming. They're coming. Miss Esperanza. Quick into your dress.

(ESPERANZA *gets up sleepily and holds out her arms.* HORTENSIA *slips on her white frilly dress and buttons it.*)

ESPERANZA: You woke me up! I was having the best dream!

HORTENSIA: May the rest of your life be a beautiful dream, *niña*. But now—hurry! *Ay quedate quieta.* This dress must have a hundred buttons.

ESPERANZA: You told me to hurry!

HORTENSIA: I told you to hurry not jump around like a cricket.

ESPERANZA: All right. I'll be a queen.

HORTENSIA: Fine *mi reina*—let's brush your hair!

(HORTENSIA *brushes out* ESPERANZA's *hair.*)

ESPERANZA: I want the red satin ribbon.

HORTENSIA: The white one is just as pretty.

ESPERANZA: You didn't iron the red one, did you!

HORTENSIA: I've been busy with your birthday.

ESPERANZA: Fine then. The white one will do. Ouch— You're pulling my hair!

HORTENSIA: *Que latosa es Usted!*

(*We hear the beginning of* Cielito Lindo. *As* HORTENSIA *ties the ribbon in* ESPERANZA's *hair.*)

ESPERANZA: They're here! Hurry up!

(*She runs to throw open the large doors to the patio. Light streams in. The three* MARIACHIS, *their black suits studded with silver, start playing and singing the traditional birthday song* Las Mañanitas. *Two Campesinos are holding poles with a banner saying "Rancho Linda Flor" with three large beautiful roses painted on it. Behind them is a crowd of campesinos in work clothes, and a little servant girl. Friends and family are there too, decked out in European style clothing.* ESPERANZA's *father,* SIXTO, *is holding two roses.* MIGUEL *beside him is holding a large brightly wrapped box.*)

ALL: *(Sing:) Estas son las mañanitas*
Que cantaba el rey David
A las muchachas bonitas
Se las cantaba asi:

Despierta mi bien, despierta
Que ya se amaneció
Y los pajaros ya cantan
La luna ya se metió.

(They end with cheers of "Happy Birthday", "Feliz Cumpleaños", and some chant, "Esperan-za!", "Esperan-za!" and clap. They all come forward with little gifts or offerings of fruit.)

ESPERANZA: Mamá, Papá—what a beautiful fiesta! You've made me very happy.

RAMONA: Then I'm happy too.

SIXTO: *(Approaches with* MIGUEL *behind him)* M'hija adorada! What a sad birthday it would be without a gift of roses! Twelve roses—one perfect rose for each precious year of your life!

ESPERANZA: Mmmmmmm. *Huele a dulce.* They smell so delicious.

(The little SERVANT GIRL *comes up and stands on tiptoe to smell them. First she looks at* SIXTO *to make sure it's all right. He nods to* ESPERANZA *who holds them out to the girl.)*

SERVANT GIRL: Mmmmmmm. *Huele a dulce. (She runs away.)*

SIXTO: Miguel. *Ven.*

*(*MIGUEL *steps forward with the package.)*

SIXTO: As I have every year since you were born—a beautiful doll for my own muñequita.

ESPERANZA: Yes! Yes!

*(*MARIELENA *approaches to see.)*

SIXTO: This year's doll comes right from Spain-Sevilla...*con mantilla Ole!*

ESPERANZA: Oooooooo.

SIXTO: This doll is the most special of any I have given you before. Do you know why?

ESPERANZA: It's the most beautiful! Its eyes open and close!

SIXTO: No. this doll is special because it is the last doll I will ever give you.

ESPERANZA: But Papá—

SIXTO: Next year you'll be thirteen. On your way to being a young woman. You won't want dolls anymore.

ESPERANZA: I'll always want dolls!

SIXTO: I'm afraid not. You'll want dresses and purses and shawls and even more ribbons for your hair. So treasure this doll—and keep it always to remember what is was like to be twelve and how much your papá loved you! Now—*todos—a divertirse!* Today is a fiesta. Dance, eat, drink, *ándale mi gente.* You too Miguelín, Doña Hortensia!

(*Some campesinos come up and kiss* SIXTO's *hand or* RAMONA's *and say "gracias patron", "gracias señor", "gracias patrona, señora". They say "felicidades señito" to* ESPERANZA.)

(SIXTO *goes to* RAMONA *and presents her with a single rose.*)

SIXTO: And you, *mi amor*, as I said since the first day I met you—I give you my life in this rose!

RAMONA: You have such good taste.

SIXTO: Yes. Of course, the good taste to fall in love forever! Shall we dance?

(*Huge platters of food are brought out. The little* SERVANT GIRL *carries a very heavy one which makes her stagger.* MIGUEL *helps her. The* MARIACHIS *play and some people dance.*)

ESPERANZA: Hortensia!

HORTENSIA: Yes, *mi reina.*

ESPERANZA: Buckle my shoes, please. My hands are shaking. I'm too excited. My *papá's* brought me a doll from Sevilla!

(HORTENSIA *shakes her head. As soon as the shoes are buckled* ESPERANZA *runs for the door where a well-dressed girl,* MARIELENA, *approaches her. The little* SERVANT GIRL *follows.*)

MARIELENA: *Felicidades* Esperanza *Felicidades*. I love your dress. So much lace. Almost like mine, oooo and a mountain of presents. You are so lucky. Let's open some!

ESPERANZA: Let's look at the doll!

(*The little* SERVANT GIRL *follows hesitantly. But she isn't noticed until they arrive at the stack of presents.* MARIELENA *turns to the girl.*)

MARIELENA: Yes? What do you want?

SERVANT GIRL: To see all the pretty things.

MARIELENA: Don't they need you in the kitchen?

(ESPERANZA *unwraps her father's present. It is a traveling chest with a beautiful doll inside.*)

MARIELENA: Ooooo look, an itty bitty comb with pearls and a white *mantilla* and gloves. Mine doesn't have gloves.

ESPERANZA: And look at all these clothes! (*She takes out dress after dress.*)

MARIELENA: What are you going to name her?

ESPERANZA: I don't know yet. I have to think of a very special name.

MARIELENA: She has real lashes on her eyes. Oooooooo. I'm so jealous!

(*The* SERVANT GIRL *reaches out to touch the dresses.*)

SERVANT GIRL: *Ayyyy, mona...que mona...*

(ESPERANZA *jerks the doll away from her,* MARIELENA *slaps the girl's hand.*)

MARIELENA: India *prieta—anda*! I told you to go to the kitchen!

(*The little girl starts to cry.* RAMONA *and* HORTENSIA *enter.*)

HORTENSIA: *Escuincle—que haces aqui?*

SERVANT GIRL: *Quise ver los regalos, no mas*

RAMONA: Girls! Shame on you. I don't think it would hurt to let her hold the doll for a few moments!

ESPERANZA: *Mamá*. This doll is special! Besides, she's poor and dirty.

HORTENSIA: *Con permiso. Señora* (*She exits with the doll.*)

RAMONA: Esperanza!

ESPERANZA: What?

RAMONA: When you scorn these people, you scorn Miguel and Hortensia. And you embarrass yourself. Now come in and receive the rest of your gifts from our gente with a smile.

ESPERANZA: *Ay mamá.* They only bring fruit. Let them put it in a bowl.

RAMONA: People give what they can. At the very least you owe them respect in return.
This life we enjoy rests on their shoulders!

ESPERANZA: No. Their life rests on ours! *Papá* made this life for us. He cleared this land with his own machete. He brought the grapes from Spain and the cattle from Brazil. He dug the roses from Sevilla and planted them here! Without us, our gente would have no work!

(TIO LUIS *enters with one pistolero.*)

ESPERANZA: Isn't that true, Tio Luis?

(ESPERANZA *laughs and starts to run off. One of* LUIS' *pistoleros stops her and points to her uncle.*)

LUIS: Don't forget your manners, young lady.

ESPERANZA: Yes Tio. Hello Tio.

LUIS: *Muchacho*—

(A pistolero brings over a large papaya.)

LUIS: I brought you this papaya from Veracruz.

ESPERANZA: Oh fruit! Thank you Tio.

LUIS: Happy birthday.

(ESPERANZA *exits.*)

LUIS: Ramona, *que hermosa te ves. Como siempre*

RAMONA: You're too kind

LUIS: My brother is a very very fortunate man. I may have the money in the family—but he...he has the treasure! *Verdad, muchachos*

(The two pistoleros chuckle and smile in agreement.)

RAMONA: Must you always bring your *pistolero*, Luis ? Certainly you have no enemies here.

LUIS: Yes-I apologize for this vermin. But, these are dangerous times. There are bandits in the hills, and—Caray, as President of the bank, one must always show one is a very serious man. In my position it is better to be feared than loved, don't you think?

RAMONA: I think you've accomplished exactly what you wish.

LUIS: Good. Good. Stay as lovely as you are, cuñada.

(LUIS *bows.* RAMONA *hurries away.* LUIS *and his men go mix with the other guests. On the way to her father* ESPERANZA *takes off her shoes. She runs, weaving through the crowd past* MIGUEL *with his mother.*)

ESPERANZA: Look Miguel. I'm a gypsy. I have no shoes!

MIGUEL: *(Pulls out her ribbon.)* Gypsies don't wear ribbons. They put flowers in their hair!

ESPERANZA: Hortensia, look what he did!

HORTENSIA: Here I'll tie it for you.

ESPERANZA: *(To* MIGUEL*)* Did you bring me a present?

MIGUEL: No.

ESPERANZA: Yes you did. Let me see! *(She tugs at his arm.)*

MIGUEL: *(Pulls something out of his pocket)* O K, *ven*. One, two—*mangos de Manila, suave y dulce como un meringue*. Your favorite!

ESPERANZA: Oh fruit! Thank you... Would you put them in a bowl, Miguelin. I can't carry them around with me right now! *(She runs off to join her father.)*

MIGUEL: She's spoiled!

HORTENSIA: She's only twelve.

MIGUEL: You were selling tortillas in the street at twelve.

HORTENSIA: *Otro mundo*. And it's time you understood it.

MIGUEL: What do you mean?

HORTENSIA: You can't go around pulling her hair any more.

MIGUEL: So what if I pull her hair?! We always kid around.

HORTENSIA: "Always" no longer exists. You're older now. So is she. You can't be friends in the same way.

MIGUEL: Are you telling me to know my place?

HORTENSIA: Yes. You are the housekeeper's son. Esperanza is the ranch owner's daughter.

MIGUEL: And?

HORTENSIA: And a deep river runs between you, Miguel. Esperanza stands on one side of this river and you on the other. And this river can never be crossed. *Me entiendes?*

MIGUEL: *Claro que sí*.

(Three vaqueros in dusty clothes rush in and over to SIXTO. *They pull him away excitedly. He listens and becomes very serious.)*

SIXTO: *Ándale pues*.

(They hurry away.)

SIXTO: Miguel! *Ven!*

MIGUEL: *A sus ordenes*.

ESPERANZA: What's wrong *papá*?

SIXTO: Nothing, *mi muñequita*. Just some trouble with the cattle! *(To* MIGUEL*)* Saddle our horses. There's trouble near the six hills!

MIGUEL: Right away, *patrón*. *(He runs off.)*

ESPERANZA: What do you mean trouble?

SIXTO: Nothing you should worry about!

ESPERANZA: I want to go with you, Papá.

SIXTO: No. Not now.

ESPERANZA: I can ride a horse too. Why does Miguel get to go, not me?

SIXTO: Because Miguel knows how to fix things and he's learning his job! Now, enjoy your party. Don't eat too many mangos. Leave some for me. You promise?

ESPERANZA: Yes *papá*.

(ESPERANZA *runs after* MIGUEL *and watches as he straps on a gun and kisses his mother.* SIXTO *hurries out. He stops and whispers something to* RAMONA.)

RAMONA: *Ay no!* Bandits! So close?!

SIXTO: *No le hagas. Soy hombre de acerro mi amor!*

RAMONA: Be careful!

(*End of Scene One*)

Scene Two

(*It is Night. The patio has been cleared. There is a huge moon. We see* RAMONA *silhouetted against it. The* MARIACHIS *are playing softly but they are invisible to the people onstage.* RAMONA *is singing the song the* MARIACHIS *are playing, she is searching the horizon. As she sings,* ESPERANZA *opens her window. She hasn't been able to sleep either.* HORTENSIA *enters and starts placing lit candles everywhere.*)

RAMONA: *Ay si la ra la ra la*
Ay, la,la,la

Vuela, vuela jilguerillo
Rayo brillante del sol
Llevate este papelito
Al dueño de mi amor.

Ay si la ra la ra la
Ay la la la

(ESPERANZA *opens her window. She sings the second verse.* RAMONA *is startled.*)

ESPERANZA: *Vuela vuela jilguerillo*
Donde tu puedes volar
A buscar mis amores
Que no los puedo olvidar

BOTH: *Ay si la ra la ra la*
Ay la,la,la

Ay si la ra la ra la
Ay la la la

RAMONA: Did my singing wake you?

ESPERANZA: No. I couldn't sleep.

RAMONA: I know. *Ven mi amor.*

(ESPERANZA *in her nightgown climbs out the window and runs to her mother. They embrace.*)

ESPERANZA: Did *papá* come home?

RAMONA: No.

ESPERANZA: *Ay.*

RAMONA: He's just a little late.

ESPERANZA: I know. But Mamá?

RAMONA: What *m'hija*?

ESPERANZA: I saw Miguel take a rifle.

RAMONA: Yes

ESPERANZA: *Papá* too?

RAMONA: Yes.

ESPERANZA: I heard Hortensia warn Miguel about the bandits. Who are the bandits?

RAMONA: They're desperate men.

ESPERANZA: Why are they desperate?

RAMONA: They have no land. They're very angry.

ESPERANZA: Are they angry with us?

RAMONA: Yes.

ESPERANZA: But they don't even know us.

RAMONA: They don't see us as people, they only see our land. They see cattle grazing on acres and acres as far as the eye can see, while some of them are forced to eat cats. Imagine. Many of these bandits hate all people who own a lot of land. They try to...to hurt them and make them leave. People say these bandits steal from the rich and give to the poor. But these men don't always give to the poor and they kill innocent people

ESPERANZA: *Papá* says we own a lot of land.

RAMONA: Yes we do. But your *papá* is a good and generous man. Our workers eat for free. And your *papá* has given them land of their own and houses. The people know that.

ESPERANZA: But do the bandits know that?

RAMONA: I hope so.

HORTENSIA: *(Enters with some candles) Señora*, is there something I can get for you?

RAMONA: No thank you.

HORTENSIA: Some candles. Surely Our Lady will see our little lights of hope.

(They light them. HORTENSIA *kneels near one of the candles and prays quietly.)*

ESPERANZA: *Mamá?*

RAMONA: Yes.

ESPERANZA: Will we lose our land?

RAMONA: No. This is our home.

(ESPERANZA *lies down on the ground, so do the* MARIACHIS.)

RAMONA: Esperanza! What are you doing?

ESPERANZA: I need to feel the land. *(She lies down.)* You lie down too, Mamá.

RAMONA: Not now, *mi amor*.

ESPERANZA: Please.

RAMONA: Why?

ESPERANZA: Because the land will speak to you. If you are very, very still and very patient you can hear its big heart beat and if you wait even longer, you can feel it breathe. *Papá* always says if you are connected to the land, you are connected to life! Lie down, Mamá! I hear something! Listen!

RAMONA: Now is not the time.
I think you need a quiet heart to hear the earth.
Now I would only hear my own heart beating.

(The MARIACHIS *get up and shrug their shoulders. They didn't hear anything. It starts to get darker.)*

(One of the MARIACHIS *taps another on his shoulder and points excitedly in the distance.)*

RAMONA: Horses! *M'hija*. Horses!

ESPERANZA: Oh. Someone's coming! *Papá! Papá!*

(RAMONA *sinks to her knees and prays silently.* ESPERANZA *joins her.)*

(*A silhouette appears against the moon walking towards them. Followed by some men. They are carrying something heavy between them. The* MARIACHIS *go quickly to see them.*)

RAMONA: Sixto? Is that you?

(MIGUEL *steps forward into the light. He carries* SIXTO's *belt and hat.*)

MIGUEL: It's me, Doña. Miguel.

RAMONA: And Sixto?

ESPERANZA: Where is *papá*?!

MIGUEL: Over there

RAMONA: *Dis mio!* Sixto, Sixto. *Mi amor, mi vida!!*...

(RAMONA *runs to the men and embraces the form they are carrying. We only see this in silhouette.* MIGUEL *and* ESPERANZA *are the only two standing in the light.*)

MIGUEL: I'm sorry.

ESPERANZA: What?

MIGUEL: I'm so sorry.
He's dead, mi reina.

(ESPERANZA *takes her father's belt and hat, covers them with kisses and starts crying.*)

ESPERANZA: Liar!

MIGUEL: It's true.

ESPERANZA: No!

MIGUEL: Yes.

ESPERANZA: Then it's your fault.

MIGUEL: I didn't kill him!

ESPERANZA: How dare you come back here alive when he's dead. How dare you show your face. You let him die. *Bestia! Cobarde!*

MIGUEL: *No, mi reina.* I didn't leave him. I loved him like a father. I would have given my life for him, but he went off on his own...and they shot him.

ESPERANZA: Shot him.

MIGUEL: Yes.

ESPERANZA: Was it the bandits, Miguel? Tell me.

MIGUEL: Yes. I'm sorry.

ESPERANZA: He lied then! *Papá* lied!
How can land mean life—if they killed my *papá* for land?!! (*She cries.*)

(End of Scene Two)

Scene Three

(The MARIACHIS *sing as a long line of workers, neighbors and the family follows* ESPERANZA *and* RAMONA *to a grassy spot near the house.* LUIS *has his two pistoleros place a heavy headstone among the roses.)*

(The workers are in their work clothes. The family is dressed very formally in black. RAMONA *and* ESPERANZA *wear heavy black mantillas.)*

(A priest sprinkles holy water on the grave. All kneel and cross themselves. The little SERVANT GIRL *cuts roses and gives them to each person present so they can place them on the grave.)*

MARIACHIS: *(Sing Corrido Of El Rancho Linda Flor)*
Here fell Don Sixto Otega
In the dust of his ranch Linda Flor.
Shot in the back by *bandidos*
Who kill the rich and rob the poor!

Ramona his widow is crying
His daughter distraught and in tears
His ranch Linda Flor in disorder
His brother Luis much too near.

*(*SERVANT GIRL *sings* Ave Maria. RAMONA *almost faints at one moment.* LUIS—*helps her to stand. She pulls away from him.* ESPERANZA *is kneeling smelling the roses.* MIGUEL *approaches.)*

ESPERANZA: Do you remember, Miguel, when papá planted these roses for us?

MIGUEL: I can never forget.

ESPERANZA: The pink ones. Like dawn for me.

MIGUEL: The red ones...

ESPERANZA: Like sunset for you

MIGUEL: We were such small children then.

ESPERANZA: *Papá* loved you like a son.

MIGUEL: But I'm not his son. See? *(He places his arm next to* ESPERANZA.*)* Soy raza de bronce, reinita*, and you—white as the best Spanish lace.

ESPERANZA: So?

MIGUEL: White is the color of money. Brown is the color of work.

ESPERANZA: But *papá* loved you—

MIGUEL: Your father was a good man. He gave us a cabin and land. Perhaps I was almost a son. But your uncle would take it all away and treat us like animals.

ESPERANZA: No! That will never happen. My *mamá* will talk to him. He listens to my mother.

MIGUEL: *Ojalá.*

(They join the crowd at the grave.)

LUIS: Are you all right?

RAMONA: As you see.

LUIS: You look so sad and pale. Grieving does not suit you. I hope you won't wear black all year.

RAMONA: Black will be my favorite color, Luis

LUIS: It doesn't need to be.
I said, it doesn't need to be.

RAMONA: What do you mean?

LUIS: Ramona, I want you to know...to know...

RAMONA: What Luis?

LUIS: You don't have to be alone. I'm here for you in all ways. In any way that would bring you happiness.

RAMONA: Be careful what you say!

LUIS: I have always loved you.

RAMONA: You're grieving. You don't know what you're saying.

LUIS: I do. I have always longed for you. You knew that. You knew that!

RAMONA: *Buitre!* You offend me!
How dare you propose with the earth still fresh over your brother's grave!

LUIS: I'm concerned for you. I love you. I'm no beast. We would wait the appropriate amount of time out of respect for my brother. One year is customary, is it not?

RAMONA: I have no desire to marry you, Luis. Now or ever.

LUIS: I see. I am wounded to the core by your words. But emotions aside, I hope you will consider my proposal from another perspective.

RAMONA: There is no other perspective.

LUIS: Actually there is. Your husband Sixto Ortega left this house and all its contents to you and your daughter. You will also receive a yearly income from the grapes.

RAMONA: I'm aware of that Luis.

LUIS: Are you aware that women cannot inherit land! Sixto left the land to me. So, if you wish to be free of the burden of my continued presence—I will purchase the house for this amount. *(He hands her some papers.)*

RAMONA: Are you mad?! This is our home. My husband meant for us to live here. And the house...is worth twenty times this much!

LUIS: Not really. I own the land the house is on. No one would dare buy it from you.

RAMONA: I would never sell it. We have no where else to live.

LUIS: I will give you a place to live.

RAMONA: The answer is still no.

LUIS: You will regret your decision, Ramona. Keep in mind that this house and those grapes are on my property. I can make things difficult for you. Very difficult. I will let you sleep on your decision—marry me or sell—both offers are more than generous!

(LUIS *exits.* RAMONA *cries.* ESPERANZA *goes to her.*)

ESPERANZA: Don't cry, *mamá*. Everything will be all right.

MARIACHIS: Here lies Don Sixto Ortega.
Shot like a dog in the back.
Red roses grow on his gravestone
His wife and his daughter in black.

Who will take care of his cattle?
Who will harvest his fields of grapes?
Who will water his red Spanish roses?
Who will be tending his grave?

(It grows dark. A blood-red quarter moon comes out. Everyone places their flowers, kisses the headstone and leaves. ESPERANZA *and* RAMONA *retire.)*

(End of Scene Three)

Scene Four

(We hear night noises. The MARIACHIS *are keeping watch perhaps carrying rifles.)*

MARIACHIS: *(Singing)* Night drops down like a black curtain
The moon is bright red in the skies
A flame leaps from torches to rooftops Don Luis smiles as everyone cries—
"Fire! Fire! Fire!"

(This cry blends into everyone crying out "Fire! Fire!" We hear horses and shouts. We see smoke and then flames.)

ESPERANZA: *Mamá*—where are you?

RAMONA: Here. Take my hand.

ESPERANZA: *Mamá*, what's happening?

RAMONA: *(Offstage)* The house is on fire! We must get out!

*(*HORTENSIA *runs in as* ESPERANZA *and* RAMONA *climb out the window.* RAMONA *trips and falls.)*

HORTENSIA: *Señora* Ortega! Esperanza!

RAMONA: Here! We're here!

HORTENSIA: Jesus, Maria, Jose!

ESPERANZA: Wait! Wait! I forgot something! *(She runs back in.)*

RAMONA: No! Esperanza. No! *(She tries to get up and cannot.)* Miguel! Esperanza's in the fire!

MIGUEL: Where? Esperanza!

ESPERANZA: Up here!

MIGUEL: The stairs are burning! *Escalera! Escalera!*

HORTENSIA: Hurry! *Ai dios todopoderoso!*

RAMONA: I have to get in there! *(She tries to walk and can't.)*

HORTENSIA: Can you get up?

RAMONA: No. Please God—I can't lose my daughter too!

*(*RAMONA *and* HORTENSIA *hold each other.* MIGUEL *comes out with* ESPERANZA *who clasps her doll in its case. They are both coughing and covered with ash.)*

RAMONA: Esperanza why did you do something so stupid! I thought I lost you too!

ESPERANZA: I had to get *Papá*'s doll. I couldn't let her burn. It's all I have of him

RAMONA: I understand. I know.

MIGUEL: The stables caught fire! *Ay* the horses! *Vámanos muchachos (He runs offstage.)*

CHORUS: *Claro! Pronto!*

(MIGUEL *runs offstage. We hear more horses.* LUIS *enters.)*

HORTENSIA: The vines! Oh the vines! Look, the whole hillside's on fire!
The rose garden is gone!
It's the end of the world!

RAMONA: We've lost everything.

LUIS: Ramona!
I was out fixing fences! I saw the smoke!
Are you alright?

RAMONA: I'm fine.

ESPERANZA: *Mamá, Mamá*
What will we do? Where will we go?

LUIS: Don't be afraid. I will take care of you both.
Come. I will help you.
Now you must stay with me.

RAMONA: Thank you Luis. But I can't leave here. My husband is here.
My life is here.

LUIS: But there's nowhere to stay. Come home with me.

RAMONA: No. Luis. We will stay in the servants' quarters. With Hortensia and Miguel.

LUIS: Of course. If you prefer.

RAMONA: I prefer.

LUIS: But...how long can you live with the servants?

RAMONA: Until I rebuild.

LUIS: You expect to rebuild?

RAMONA: Yes. Of course.

LUIS: But *cuñada*—where will you get the money to rebuild? The house is gone. The vineyards have burned to the ground. You are destitute. You have nothing.
I will not pressure you to marry me, but I must beg you to consider it. Right now you are only thinking of yourself, which is understandable. But you

must think of others. Think of your gente who depend on you for their livelihood. Think of your darling daughter. Sixto worked so very hard...you might say he gave his life so you two would be

cherished and protected.
Do you think he would want anything less now when you need it most?

ESPERANZA: *Mamá?!*

RAMONA: Quiet. Let me think.

LUIS: A word from you—can make everyone's life easier...or not.

RAMONA: I see.
Yes Luis, I will consider your proposal.

ESPERANZA: *Mamá*, no!

LUIS: I have no doubt that you will make the right decision. Although you don't love me, my heart is yours! I will be back in the morning for your answer. *(He starts to leave.)*

ESPERANZA: *(To* LUIS*)* I hate you!

LUIS: And Ramona, if Esperanza is to be my daughter, she must learn better manners. In fact, today I will look into boarding schools where they can teach her to act like a young lady. *(He exits.)*

ESPERANZA: *Mamá*, why? Why did you tell him that?

RAMONA: I know what I'm doing. I will never marry that man. I have money in the bank.

HORTENSIA: His bank.

RAMONA: Friends will help.

HORTENSIA: And pay with their lives.

RAMONA: You are right. You are right.

HORTENSIA: *Ay señora*. The truth is—if you stay here, you will be destitute. You will have to marry Don Luis.

RAMONA: I don't know what to do. *(She tries to walk and can't.)* I think my ankle is broken.

ESPERANZA: I'll help you, *mamá*.

RAMONA: My ankle is the least of our problems. The bone can be fixed by a doctor.
This situation can only be fixed by me. Our lives *and* the lives of everyone around us are depending on my decision.

HORTENSIA: *Doña* Ramona. There's something you should know.

RAMONA: Yes?

HORTENSIA: Don't sacrifice yourself for us. Miguel and I have decided to go to the United States. My brother Alfonso has been writing to us about the big farm in California where he works now. He can arrange jobs and a cabin for us.

ESPERANZA: You're deserting us too?!

MIGUEL: We have his letter. Proof of work will allow us to cross the border.

RAMONA: When are you leaving?

HORTENSIA: Tonight, *si dios quiere.*

RAMONA: What if Esperanza and I went with you to the United States?

ESPERANZA: Mamá— We can't just leave!

RAMONA: What should we do Esperanza? Do you want me to marry *Tio* Luis and let him send you far away from me?

ESPERANZA: No.

RAMONA: Hortensia, what do you think?

HORTENSIA: *Doña,* I don't know.

MIGUEL: There's only field work there. Hard, dirty work.

RAMONA: I'm not afraid of work.

MIGUEL: Doña, with all due respect—you can't travel with a broken ankle. You can't work, and worse, they might stop us at the border because of you.

RAMONA: I have thought of that, Miguel. Let me speak to Esperanza for a moment.
Anza, come here. Are you feeling strong?

ESPERANZA: Yes.

RAMONA: You are strong! *Conste!*

ESPERANZA: *Si,* Mamá.

RAMONA: You're only twelve. But twelve will have to be old enough. We are going to be like that beautiful bird, the phoenix, that dives into the fire and rises, re-born from its ashes. We will rise again—with a new life ahead of us—in California with Hortensia and Miguel.

ESPERANZA: All right.

RAMONA: Good. Because you will go first.

ESPERANZA: What do you mean me? What about you?

RAMONA: My ankle is broken. I can't travel. You must go without me for now.

ESPERANZA: No, no, no, no, no, no, no! Don't send me away, *mamá*. Please, please don't.
I'll be good. I promise. I swear. I'll be nice to Tio Luis. Whatever you want. I promise.

RAMONA: You will go first. The nuns at La Gloriosa will care for me until my ankle heals. Then I'll come find you with enough money so we all can live well.

HORTENSIA: Don Luis is *muy macho*. He'll never let you leave.

RAMONA: He won't find me.
He'll believe I fled with you.

ESPERANZA: No, no, no, no, no! I'll stay at the convent with you!

RAMONA: Hiding one is difficult enough. Hiding two is impossible! Hortensia, you know my life is my beautiful daughter. Can I trust you with my life?

HORTENSIA: Always. *Que Diós nos bendiga.*

MIGUEL: *Mamá*—Esperanza has never worked a day in her life. She can't even braid her own hair. She'll be nothing but trouble.

HORTENSIA: Miguel!

MIGUEL: If she goes, I will not be her servant. Remember that! *(He stomps off and goes to SIXTO's grave. He takes out a knife and viciously stabs the earth again and again.)*

ESPERANZA: *Mamá*, how can I live without you?

RAMONA: Are you living without *papá*?

ESPERANZA: Yes. But I carry him in my heart and in my head.

RAMONA: And I will think of you and I will pray for you every minute of every day and every night until we are together again.

ESPERANZA: How will I know when you're coming?

RAMONA: I will be there before you know it! I will write you whenever I can.

ESPERANZA: Please get well. Please come to me soon.

RAMONA: I promise.

HORTENSIA: Doña, the cart is ready. Miguel! Miguelín!

(MIGUEL is still furiously cutting the earth.)

MARIACHIS: *(Singing* La Rosita, *folksong)*

Cuando se mueren las rosas
Queda muy triste el jardin
Queda muy triste el jardin
Cuando se mueren las flores

Mueren las horas dichosas
Y ya no huele a jazmin
Y ya no huele a jazmin
Ni vuelan las mariposas.

When the roses die
The garden seems so sad
The garden seems so sad
When the flowers die.

The joy-filled hours die
And the scent of jasmine fades
And the scent of roses fades
And I can only cry.
Y ya no huele a jazmin
Ni vuelan las mariposas.

(End of Scene Four)

Scene Five

(Two soldiers in uniform, one Mexican, one American, march in carrying a huge banner that reads, "The Border". They stop center stage and secure it. Two bureaucrats carrying flags enter. One Mexican, one American. As they enter we hear each country's National anthem. They set up small desks and secure the flags. They salute each other, take out a huge pestle to stamp with and sit down.)

(Two of the MARIACHIS *run in out of breath. The other one is half in and half out of a "costal". He gets out and bows to a pretty young woman and hands her the costal. The three tiptoe with much fanfare past the bureaucrats—of course no one sees them. They are free to move back and forth at will. Throughout the scene, they watch all the people passing, tip their hats at pretty ladies, steal from the vendors, peek at the bureaucrat papers etc.)*

(A long line forms on the Mexican side waiting to cross the border. A few people on the American side are waiting to cross into Mexico. There are vendors on both sides, people looking for relatives etc. An obviously poor family, a mother, a father and a little boy enter on the American side. They are displaced "Okies". The father begins to play a harmonica or a violin and the little boy does an awkward dance and sings. The mother passes a hat.)

(One of the MARIACHIS *does a short riff on his trumpet when someone passes into Mexico. The other two pull him along.)*

AGENT: American Nationals! Let 'em pass! Welcome home! *(Etc)*

ESPERANZA: Hortensia, I'm soooo hot.

HORTENSIA: We can take some of this off now, I think.

MIGUEL: *Híjole. Que monton de gente!*

AGENT: *(To woman at head of the line)* You want to make trouble? Make trouble in Mexico. Go back where you belong.

WOMAN: We have papers! We live there!

AGENT: *(Tearing up her papers)* What papers?

MIGUEL: *Mamá,* We have to be careful. Any little thing you do wrong up there and they throw you back. We have to do something about Esperanza. The papers say she is my sister but she looks nothing like us. They'll stop us. They won't let us cross!

HORTENSIA: I know what to do!

(HORTENSIA *braids* ESPERANZA's *hair.*)

ESPERANZA: Stop that. I hate braids!

MIGUEL: Shhhhhh.

HORTENSIA: I'm sorry, *niña*—I have to do this

MIGUEL: *Mamá* her dress is too nice.

HORTENSIA: *(Rips off the hem of* ESPERANZA's *dress so it is too short)* I have to make it look like you borrowed it.

ESPERANZA: Why? Why?

MIGUEL: Reinita. You must calm down. If the guards see you cry. They may stop us and ask too many questions.

HORTENSIA: Talk to no one. Pretend you are mute!

MIGUEL: And whatever you do, don't cry and call attention to yourself! We are trusting you with our lives, *entiendes*?

ESPERANZA: Yes.

MIGUEL: She still doesn't look my sister.

HORTENSIA: Wait!
I must do this.

(HORTENSIA *takes up a handful of dirt and rubs it on* ESPERANZA's *skin.*)

ESPERANZA: No!

HORTENSIA: We have to!

ESPERANZA: I look like a beggar!

MIGUEL: Your skin is too white.

ESPERANZA: *Papá* would be ashamed of me!

HORTENSIA: *Muchachita*— It's a disguise. So you will be safe and come with us. Let's pretend this is the most beautiful powder for your face.

ESPERANZA: It's dirt.
You and Miguel are clean. *(She starts to cry.)*

(An obviously wealthy American woman and her daughter come by. They are handing out candy to the poor children. The MARIACHIS *notice them and run over to get a piece of candy too. Then they get in line behind* ESPERANZA. *The American couple stop in front of* ESPERANZA.*)*

AMERICAN WOMAN: Would you like a piece of candy, dear? I know your *mama* can't afford it. Here.

*(*ESPERANZA *draws herself up to refuse, but* MIGUEL *grabs it and hands it to her.)*

AMERICAN WOMEN: These people! They don't even say thank you! *(She walks off.)* Why do I bother?!

ESPERANZA: *(Handing the candy back to* MIGUEL*)* You keep the candy!

MIGUEL: Sure.
What's wrong Anza?

ESPERANZA: She felt sorry for me!
She thought I was poor.

MIGUEL: Good. Your disguise is working perfectly!

AGENT: Next! *(He examines their papers. Looks them up and down. To* HORTENSIA.*)* What's in that bag?

HORTENSIA: Our papers, *señor*.

AGENT: I see you have papers. Empty your bag.

*(*HORTENSIA *empties the bag. The* AGENT *looks over everything, points to the doll case.)*

AGENT: And that?

HORTENSIA: It's...it's only a doll.

AGENT: *(He opens it.)* Where did you get something like this!

HORTENSIA: It belongs to her. To my daughter.

MIGUEL: My sister.

ESPERANZA: Yes. Yes...the...the...lady of the house where we worked didn't want it anymore. She said I could have it.

AGENT: She did?

ESPERANZA: Yes... She was very nice. It was my birthday.

AGENT: *(Losing interest)* Good. Good. Good. Mexican Nationals—let 'em pass!

(They cross the border. The Okie family is still performing. MIGUEL *hands the candy to the little boy—who gobbles it down.)*

ESPERANZA: Are we through?

HORTENSIA: *(Crossing herself)* He didn't bother to look at our papers!

MIGUEL: The future is ours! *Arriba y adelante.*

OKIE BOY: *(Singing, he dances.)*
Many days you have lingered all around my cabin door
Oh hard times come a-gain no more.
Oh hard times come a-gain no more.

(The MARIACHIS...*strike up a welcome as* HORTENSIA, MIGUEL *and* ESPERANZA *pass to the other side.)*

ESPERANZA: This is America?

END OF ACT ONE

ACT TWO

SceneOne

(*The* MARIACHIS, ESPERANZA *holding her doll,* HORTENSIA *and* MIGUEL *are on a bus center stage. We see a backdrop of countryside that moves quickly past them. They stay still.*)

MARIACHI 1: The beautiful State of California!

MARIACHI 2: The valley of San Joaquin! Land of plenty.

MARIACHI 3: Plenty of work. Ahuuaaa!

ALL: (*Sing*) We smell oranges from a nearby grove
Flowers bloom on the trees
Melons dot the open field
Brown people on their knees.

ESPERANZA: Look at all of them working in that field. There must be a hundred people. Two hundred.

MIGUEL: At least three hundred. Four hundred!

MARIACHI 1: Not just brown people!

MARIACHI 2: Poor people. All of them.

MARIACHI 1: *La pobreza... Es triste, no?*

MARIACHI 3: (*Sing*) Esperanza, Esperanza
Is it hard to be believed?
Mexico is like water spilled
It cannot be retrieved!

(*They arrive at the camp. People start to enter, some dropping from the sky, some walking on. As they sing they assemble the camp or go about tasks like washing clothes in tubs, sweeping etc. Men walk by with heavy baskets of peaches which is the crop in season now. A little girl,* ISABEL, *dressed in a man's undershirt runs in rolling a tire. She crashes into* ESPERANZA *who drops her doll.* ISABEL *goes to help pick her up.*)

ISABEL: I'm sorry. I'm sorry.

ESPERANZA: Don't you touch her!

(MODESTA *and* ALFONSO *enter behind her.* ALFONSO *runs to* HORTENSIA *and hugs her.*)

ALFONSO: Hermana!

HORTENSIA: Alfonso!

ALFONSO: *(Embraces* HORTENSIA*) Oye hermana—que gordita éstas!*

HORTENSIA: *Y tu, que palillo!*

ALFONSO: Miguelito? *Hombre*—you look like a grown man.

HORTENSIA: Esperanza. This is my brother, Alfonso. He worked for Señor Rodriguez.

ESPERANZA: Our neighbor Señor Rodriguez?

HORTENSIA: Yes. And this is the girl I wrote you about.

ESPERANZA: Did you know Señor Rodriguez's daughter, Marielena. She was my best friend!

ALFONSO: No Esperanza. I was a field servant. I didn't know the family.

ESPERANZA: Oh.

HORTENSIA: And Modesta?

ALFONSO: With the new baby!!
Our home is to the right. Bienvendos. Welcome home.

(*The adults shake hands and embrace. Talk among themselves as they go to their cabin.* ESPERANZA *is cool to* ISABEL, *but* ISABEL *shows her the camp. People comment as the girls pass.*)

ESPERANZA: What is that shack?

ISABEL: That's where we live.

ESPERANZA: Our horses had better stalls than that!

ISABEL: Wow!
You'll like this camp. It has good water. All the toilets are over there.

ESPERANZA: So far away?

ISABEL: In some camps we had to go in ditches!
You'll love our fiestas! We have them every Saturday night. There is music and food and dancing. I can't wait! Can you dance?

ESPERANZA: Of course.

(*A man, one of the* MARIACHIS, *drags a large bag with mail in it. He rings a bell.*)

MAILMAN: Mail! Mail! *Paquetes y correo!*

ESPERANZA: Do you get mail here?

ISABEL: Oh yes!
Tia Hortensia used to write all the time...about you!

MAILMAN: *(As he calls names people come running out.)* Enrique Arellano. Teofilo Balendrano Josefina Cruz Valencia Faustino Garcia Flores. *Cartas de tus amores!* *(He moves on ringing his bell.)*

(They stop in front of one of the shacks. MODESTA *comes out the door and greets everyone.)*

MODESTA: *Hola.* You must be Esperanza. I'm Modesta, Isabel's mother. *Bienvenida niña.* I hope you'll feel at home here. Isabel will you show you where to put your things.

*(*MIGUEL *enters.)*

MIGUEL: Tia, do you have some of those big tomato cans?

MODESTA: Isabel—get one of the cans for Miguel.

(A baby cries as ISABEL *exits, followed by* MIGUEL.*)*

MIGUEL: I need two.

ISABEL: Mamá, Carlito's crying.

MODESTA: I'll change Carlitos.
Isabel—bring Esperanza her box!

*(*ISABEL *re-enters lugging a big cardboard box.)*

ISABEL: I'm back. This is your box for all your things. I have one of my own. We keep them under the bed.

ESPERANZA: Where's my room?

ISABEL: Here. You sleep with me.

ESPERANZA: In one bed?

ISABEL: I sleep with my head on this end and you sleep with your head on the other.

ESPERANZA: We sleep in the same bed?

ISABEL: Don't tell me you had your own bed?! Wow!

*(*ESPERANZA *takes out her clothes from the sack puts them in the box.)*

ISABEL: Why didn't you bring any of your pretty dresses?

ESPERANZA: They burned.

ISABEL: Oh. But you did have pretty dresses?

ESPERANZA: Many.

ISABEL: Did you really always get your own way and have all the dolls and fancy dresses you wanted?

ESPERANZA: What?

ISABEL: Aunt Hortensia and Miguel wrote all about you. I'm happy you're my cousin. I've never had a rich cousin.

ESPERANZA: I'm not your cousin.

ISABEL: Yes. Now you are. My *mamá* told me to call you cousin. Is your doll all right?

ESPERANZA: Yes.

ISABEL: Can I see her?

ESPERANZA: No. She's sleeping.

ISABEL: Oh.

ESPERANZA: *(Singing softly)*
A la ruru nia
Duérmaseme ya
Que si no, el coco
Se le comerá.

(ISABEL *reaches to open the box.*)

ESPERANZA: I told you not to touch her. No one can touch her but me. Entiendes? It was my father's dying wish.

ISABEL: Okay.

ESPERANZA: ...and ummmm...little girl?

ISABEL: My name's Isabel.

ESPERANZA: Isabel, yes, look—I'm tying a ribbon around the box in a special way, so if you untie it, I'll know!

HORTENSIA: Esperanza. It's your turn to take a bath!

ESPERANZA: At last! *Que divino!* (*She stands up near* HORTENSIA, *turns around puts her hands out from her sides and waits.*)

ISABEL: Esperanza, what are you doing?

ESPERANZA: Hortensia helps me with my bath. Don't you Hortensia?

ISABEL: Tía— You really help Esperanza take a bath like I do with itty bitty Carlitos? *Ay ay ay!*

ISABEL: *(Holds out her arms)* Tia, help me with my bath too!

HORTENSIA: No. no. No more helping. Don't you think that you both are old enough to take a bath by yourselves?

ESPERANZA: *(Quickly drops her arms.)* Yes. Of course.

HORTENSIA: Isabel—go and tell your mother we need more hot water.

ISABEL: *(Tiptoes out)* Okay! But I'll be back. Then you can tell me stories about what it was like to be rich. *(She exits to get* HORTENSIA.*)*

ESPERANZA: *(Yells after her)* I'm still rich. This is only temporary. Hortensia!

HORTENSIA: What, *mi amor*?

ESPERANZA: Hortensia. Nothing is right here! I can't live here! It... It's not clean...and the people don't look trustworthy. *Papá* would never let us live here! *Mamá* would never approve.

HORTENSIA: As difficult as it is to accept, our lives are different now.

ESPERANZA: Can't we have a house to ourselves?

HORTENSIA: This is a family camp. We must have a male head of household to live and work here. And that is Alfonso. He and his family went to a lot of trouble to make sure we had this cabin!

ESPERANZA: I don't care. I don't like it.

HORTENSIA: Do you know how lucky you are? Most people wait months for a job and a roof over their heads. Please be grateful for the favors bestowed on us.

ESPERANZA: How can I be grateful?! I don't even have a bed to call my own! We're all crowded in here in one shack! We're living like horses.

HORTENSIA: That's enough. Sit down.

ESPERANZA: What?

HORTENSIA: Sit down. Sit. Now listen carefully. If you had stayed in Mexico and your mother had married Don Luis—you would have had one choice—to be separated and to be miserable. Here you have two choices. To be together and be miserable or to be together and be happy! Your mother will join us soon. We have jobs, we have a roof over our heads. I choose to be happy! And you?

ESPERANZA: *(Angrily)* Happy.

HORTENSIA: Good. *(She exits.)*

*(*ESPERANZA *cries.* MIGUEL *enters.)*

MIGUEL: What's the matter, Anza?

ESPERANZA: Nothing.

MIGUEL: Nothing eh? Good. You can help me.

ESPERANZA: With what?

MIGUEL: Shhhh. I have a surprise.

ESPERANZA: I'm not helping unless I know what it is.

MIGUEL: Let me show you something. *(He takes her by the hand and leads her to a little spot where there are three large cans that seem empty and a half broken statue of the Madonna.)* I'm making a garden.

ESPERANZA: This is a poor garden.

MIGUEL: Look in the cans.

ESPERANZA: There's just dirt.

MIGUEL: There will be roses. Lots and lots and lots of roses—and all of them from Linda Flor.

ESPERANZA: But our garden was burned.

MIGUEL: Just the top. I found the roots were alive. So I brought them. And planted them. Just for us.

ESPERANZA: Ay Miguel.

MIGUEL: You think you are the only one missing home? I miss it too. I miss the ranch and Mexico and your *papa* and your *mama*—everyone.
So now you'll help me with the roses, no?
If I have to work, help me keep them in the sun, but don't let them dry out.

ESPERANZA: I will help.

HORTENSIA: *(Offstage.)* Miguel! *Ven acá!*

MIGUEL: *Voy, mamá! (He exits.)*

ESPERANZA: *Ay Mamá, mamá.*

(RAMONA *appears at the convent. Perhaps there is a large cross behind her— or a stained glass window. They can't see each other.* RAMONA *sings the* Jilguerillo *song in English.* ESPERANZA *joins in a duet with her mother and sings it in Spanish.)*

RAMONA: *Vuela, vuela jilguerillo*
donde tu puedes volar
A buscar a mis amores
Que no los puedo olvidar.

ESPERANZA: Fly fly little goldfinch
Where you alone can fly
Seek out my loved ones
Whom I think of tonight.

RAMONA & ESPERANZA: *Ay si la ra la la la*
Ay la la la

(End of Scene One)

Scene Two

(Morning. The camp. People rushing around getting ready for work. MODESTA *is hanging wash. One* MARIACHI *passes carrying a heavy load of peaches. The other two run in quickly with a banner that says "Peach Season" and has pictures of peaches in piles and peaches falling from a tree. They quickly set up the banner and then run offstage to get some empty baskets and straw hats etc. Women pass wearing aprons and bandanas.)*

*(*MIGUEL *exits the cabin with* ALFONSO. *He is putting on a clean shirt and has combed his wet hair back.)*

MIGUEL: *Tio,* How do I look?

ALFONSO: Handsome like me. *Verdad,* Tensa?

HORTENSIA: *Ay si, como no!*

*(*ESPERANZA *enters.)*

MIGUEL: See you, *mi reina!* *(He runs out. Kissing* HORTENSIA *as he exits.)*

ESPERANZA: Where is Miguel going?

HORTENSIA: He's applying for a job as a mechanic at the railroad.
A real job. My boy can fix anything with a motor.
Your father would be so proud.

ESPERANZA: Where are you going?

HORTENSIA: To work. Modesta and I will be packing peaches in the shed.

ESPERANZA: What do I do?

HORTENSIA: You stay here and help Isabel with the baby.

ESPERANZA: I want to work with you!

HORTENSIA: You're not old enough to work in the shed and Isabel isn't old enough to watch the baby by herself.

ESPERANZA: I never held a baby in my life.

HORTENSIA: Isabel will show you...and Esperanza.

ESPERANZA: Yes?

HORTENSIA: You have a camp job too—sweeping the wooden platform. You'll get paid for this.

ESPERANZA: I'll earn money?

HORTENSIA: *Bueno*—instead of paying you directly, the owners will deduct some money from our rent each month.

(MODESTA *enters singing to her baby, Carlitos.*)

MODESTA: *Señora Santana*
Porque llores el nino?
Por una manzana
Que se le ha perdido!

(*A bell rings loudly.*)

MODESTA: *Ay,* we have to go...
Mi gordito precioso... How I hate to leave you! I miss you so much!

(MODESTA *kisses him all over.* ISABEL *comes to take him.* MODESTA *has trouble handing him over.*)

MODESTA: Don't put a diaper on after his bath. He gets a rash. And make sure you mash the bananas so there's no chunks. And don't leave him to cry and cry. He only cries when he needs something. All right?

ISABEL: Yes *mama*! Don't worry.

(*One last kiss and* MODESTA *exits with* HORTENSIA.)

ISABEL: *Señora Santana.*
Porque Llores el niño? Come on—sing to him Esperanza. Make him smile.

ESPERANZA: No.

ISABEL: You sing to your doll.

ESPERANZA: I don't like babies. I'm scared of them.

ISABEL: Go mash half a banana for him.
Si Carlitos? How delicious—a ba-na-na!

ESPERANZA: Where's the banana?

ISABEL: On the table.

ESPERANZA: Where do you keep a bowl?

ISABEL: On the shelf.

ESPERANZA: What do I mash it with?

ISABEL: *Ay,* a fork!

ESPERANZA: What if I leave chunks and he chokes?

ISABEL: Don't you know how to mash a banana?

(ESPERANZA *shrugs.*)

ISABEL: All right. The diaper pail is over there. Get the soap bar and...

ESPERANZA: Where's the soap?

ISABEL: Esperanza, don't you know anything?

ESPERANZA: I know *a lot*. I went to private school starting at four so I have already passed through level eight. When my mother comes, I will go to high school!

ISABEL: I'm going to start school too—but here we learn in English.

ESPERANZA: Oh.

ISABEL: And when I go to school next week, you will be alone with the baby. What will you do?

ESPERANZA: Maybe my *mamá* will be here to show me.

ISABEL: I better teach you—in case she doesn't come. Maybe today you should start with the platform. You can sweep the floor, can't you?

ESPERANZA: Of course. Get me the broom.

ISABEL: You get it. It's over there.
Señora Santana, *porque llores el niño, Por una manzaza, Que se le ha perdido.*
(She exits singing to the baby.)

(ESPERANZA *gets the broom. She goes to the platform and starts to sweep but she doesn't know how and it flies through the air. She tries different ways and dust gets in her nose and she starts coughing and sneezing.* MAILMAN *enters ringing his bell.)*

MAILMAN: Mail! Mail!
Paquetes y correo!
Jesus Posadas
Nicolas Salmeron
Juanita Chavez Reynoso
Manuela...Manuela...Gutierrez Orozco...

ESPERANZA: Do you have a letter for me?

MAILMAN: Did I call you out?

ESPERANZA: No.

MAILMAN: Then no. *(He moves on.)* Mail! Mail!
Paquetes y correo!

(MARTA *enters and goes to the cabin door.)*

MARTA: *(Calls)* Mode! Mode!

(ISABEL *enters.)*

ISABEL: Marta—shhhhhh. The baby is sleeping. *Mamá's* at work.

MARTA: I brought your *mama* some flyers.

ISABEL: *(Sounding out a word.)* Str...rike. Strike!

MARTA: Shhh quiet.

ISABEL: She's all right. She's from Aguascalientes too! *El rancho* Linda Flor.

MARTA: Is that a town?

ESPERANZA: No it's a ranch.

ISABEL: Her father owned it and thousands and thousands of acres of land. Her name is Esperanza. This is my real cousin Marta! Esperanza had lots of servants and beautiful dresses and she went to private school. Our cousin Miguel and his mother worked for them.

MARTA: Ahh I see—a princess come to be a peasant.

ISABEL: A fire burned her house and everything! Now she has to work like us. She's nice. Her *papá* died.

MARTA: So? My father died too. Before he came to this country he fought in the Mexican Revolution against people like her father—people who owned all the land.

ESPERANZA: You know nothing about my *papa*! He was a good kind man!

MARTA: Well just so you know, this isn't Mexico. No one will be waiting on you here, Cinderella! Are you learning the skills you need to be a good servant?

ESPERANZA: I don't need to learn them...I

ISABEL: She was teaching me! Watch! *(She is really teaching* ESPERANZA *how to sweep.)* Now, I hold the broom like this. One hand here, the other hand... here. Then you I mean...I pull it. I use small strokes. All in one direction. If the dust flies around too much, I sprinkle it with water—not too much or you'll...I'll make mud. Now I get all the dirt in a pile and hold the broom down here and push it onto this piece of cardboard. I find if you wet the edge, the dirt goes in better. Is that how you do it too Esperanza?

ESPERANZA: *(Taking the broom)* Yes. All the time.
You are doing very, very well. And Isabel....

ISABEL: What?

ESPERANZA: *Gracias prima.* Thank you for your help.

(MIGUEL *enters.*)

ISABEL: Miguel! Miguel! Do you have a day off already?!
Pick me up!

MIGUEL: Not now, Isabel.

ESPERANZA: What are you doing back so soon Miguel? Didn't they have a job at the railroad?

MIGUEL: Sure, if I wanted to lay tracks and dig ditches! They don't want Mexicanos as mechanics! I might as well work in the fields!

ESPERANZA: I'm so sorry,

MIGUEL: It's not your fault, *mi reina*.

ISABEL: Oooooooo, he called you *"mi reina"* my queen. I want to be a queen too! *(She runs around making queenly poses.)* I'm a queen. I'm a queen. *La reina Hermosa*...I'm a queen, Marta, Marta. I'm a queen. I'm a queen!

MARTA: *(To* MIGUEL*) Mi reina*? I didn't know servants in Mexico could talk like that to their *patronas*.

MIGUEL: What business is it of yours? Who are you?

MARTA: Hi. I'm Marta Carranza. Modesta's my aunt too.
You should read this flyer!

MIGUEL: Marta. Marta... Yes. You're the one organizing the workers!

MARTA: Yes. Shhhhh!

MIGUEL: My uncle says you'll cause us trouble.

MARTA: *Tio* Alfonso is a frightened man.

MIGUEL: Frightened for his family. We didn't come here for trouble. We came here to work.

MARTA: What good does it do to work, if you can't live on what you make!

ESPERANZA: They have nothing. Even a little is better than nothing.

MARTA: They? They? It's "we" now, Cinderella. Thousands of Mexicanos. We can't wait here helpless like sheep standing in line for the slaughter. We are thousands. We have power.

MIGUEL: What power? Hunger isn't power!

MARTA: Our work is power! Our hands, our backs, out minds! If we strike, if we stop working- the bosses will have no one to plant their food, clean their homes, dig their ditches, drive their trucks, take care of their children. If we take all that away from them, they'll have to pay us more, give us running water, electricity and decent homes!

(We hear a truck pull up. Men, including the MARIACHIS, *dirty from the fields file through.)*

ISABEL: Oh-oh Marta, *Papá* is home.

MIGUEL: If we strike, we lose our jobs. It's that simple.

MARTA: You're new. You'll learn.
Listen, I shouldn't be telling you this, but the strikers are more organized then they appear. In a little while things are going to happen all over the county. We're going to shut down everything, the fields, the sheds, the railroad!

MIGUEL: The railroad?

MARTA: Everything!

MIGUEL: And a lot of people are joining this strike?

MARTA: A multitude!
If you have not joined us by then, be very careful! If you're not with us, you're against us! That's how we think.

ISABEL: Oh-oh!

(ALFONSO *enters*.)

ALFONSO: Marta *que milagro*. What's up?

MARTA: *Tio*. Aren't you glad to see me?

ALFONSO: I don't want you preaching the strike to my family.

MARTA: It's a free country. I can say what I want.

ALFONSO: Say it somewhere else. We don't want to be sent back to Mexico with you when you're caught.

MARTA: They can't send me back! I was born here. I am one hundred percent *puritita* Americana—whether they like it or not! I've never even been to Mexico.

ALFONSO: Then think of the rest of us! We need to work! If we cause trouble—we have nothing. If we work hard, we keep our jobs, we make a future!

MARTA: What future, Tio? Hundreds of truckloads of poor white people come every day. If we work for four cents, they'll work for three! What future do we have with people like that?

ALFONSO: I think it is time you went home, Marta. I will tell Mode you came by!

MARTA: You better watch out Tio. The line is drawn. Strikers against those who do not support us. Be very careful. We can get violent with those who stand in our way! Watch your back. *(Calls out as she leaves)* *Venceremos*! We will win!

ALFONSO: Marta will get us all into trouble.

MIGUEL: The strike may be a good thing.

ALFONSO: Don't you start.

MIGUEL: *Tranquilo,* Tio. It's not what you think. If so many workers are joining the strikes, I might be able to get a job at the railroad after all.

ESPERANZA: But if there's a strike and the rest of us lose our jobs? How will we live?

MIGUEL: "We"? All of a sudden it's "we"?

ESPERANZA: Yes. "We". The family. Our...our people.

ISABEL: Will we be sent back to Mexico, Papá?

ALFONSO: Not on my watch! *(He picks up* ISABEL *and they exit.)* Ayyy—you weigh more than...a sack of peaches!

ISABEL: A sack of...of asparagus?

ALFONSO: Much, much more! A sack of potatoes!

ESPERANZA: I don't like Marta! Didn't you see how rude she was?

MIGUEL: Yes. She is angry.

ESPERANZA: How could you even talk to her?

MIGUEL: I respect her. Unlike you, Señorita, I understand her anger!

(End of Scene Two)

Scene Three

(Morning. ALFONSO *and* HORTENSIA *drinking coffee on the porch of their cabin.* ESPERANZA *enters. She gives them a plate of food.)*

MARIACHIS: *(Sing)* We sing now for Esperanza.
Waiting each day for the mail.
Three weeks, now four weeks have gone by
And there is no letter still.
Each day she rises at sunrise
Hope with the new light is born.
But where is her mother? How is she?
Why does she leave her alone?

HORTENSIA: *Felicidades* Esperanza. Your first breakfast is delicious!

ALFONSO: Yes. Heaven must smell like this meal!

ESPERANZA: It's only *frijoles.*

ALFONSO: But what *frijoles!*

HORTENSIA: I'm so proud of you!

ESPERANZA: The ones on the bottom are burnt.

ALFONSO: But the ones on top—*esquisitos!*
And you made the *tortillas!*

ESPERANZA: Yes.

(MIGUEL *enters with a tortilla.*)

MIGUEL: This one looks more like a *tostada* than a *tortilla.*

(ALFONSO *puts on his sombrero to go to work.*)

ALFONSO: As luck would have it—I adore *tostadas!*
Isabel! *Apúrate!* Your cousin is ready to take you to the school bus!

MIGUEL: Not today, Tio.

ALFONSO: No?

MIGUEL: I can't.

ALFONSO: Why? What's her name?

ESPERANZA: Who?

ALFONSO: His new girlfriend. The one who put that smile on his face and is keeping him from taking his adoring cousin to the school bus!

MIGUEL: What girlfriend? I'm going to the railroad. They're hiring extra people in case there's a strike. I'll have a chance to work on the engines. I know it might be temporary, but if I do a good job, maybe they will keep me.

ALFONSO: That is right. You do good work. They will see it. They will keep you! You see. This is America.

(ISABEL *comes running in and goes up to* MIGUEL.)

ISABEL: Take me to school. I command it!

MIGUEL: So you're a queen today giving orders. Is that why you have little gold stars stuck all over your face?

ISABEL: My teacher gave me five gold stars on my English spelling test.
I did the best in the whole class.

MIGUEL: And you put them on your face?

ISABEL: So everyone can see.

MIGUEL: *Que sangrona eres!* (*He gives her a kiss.*) *Adíos!*

ISABEL: Miguel!

(HORTENSIA *and* MODESTA *enter, dressed for work.* MODESTA *carries Cariltos.*)

ALFONSO: Forget Miguel! Today's your lucky day. I'm taking you to the bus!

(*The* MAILMAN *enters.*)

MAILMAN: Mail, mail. *Paquetes y correo* Emiliano Toto Urbano
Andres Aguirre Chacha
Maria Chuchena—*una bella azucena*
Narciso Ochoa Ramon
Five letters from your home!

(ESPERANZA *approaches.*)

MAILMAN: Sorry *niña*, nothing for you. Mail, mail *paquetes y correo!*

(MAILMAN *exits. Two* MARIACHIS *follow* ESPERANZA *who walks slowly to the porch.* MARIACHIS *sing.*)

(ESPERANZA *goes to the garden. There are flowers blooming in the cans. She waters them and smells them and kneels before the virgin and prays silently.* HORTENSIA *enters.*)

ESPERANZA: Hortensia!

HORTENSIA: You made a good breakfast today.

ESPERANZA: Hortensia. I haven't heard from my mother in three months!

HORTENSIA: I know. I know.

ESPERANZA: Do you think she's alright?

HORTENSIA: If anything very bad had happened, we would know. Bad news travels fast.

ESPERANZA: I hope so.

HORTENSIA: She is a good mother. She loves you with a thousand hearts. She will come as soon as she can.

ESPERANZA: And if I am a good daughter, I should go and get her.

HORTENSIA: But how? With what money? I would gladly loan you, but we barely have enough for us all.

ESPERANZA: I would never ask you for money. I can work. I can work. I can work and save money to go back and bring *mamá* here.

HORTENSIA: Modesta can't afford to pay you, *m'hija.*

ESPERANZA: No, no, no. I will find work in the shed. With you.

HORTENSIA: You're too young.

ESPERANZA: I can look older. See? (*She holds up her hair.*)

(MODESTA *enters.*)

MODESTA: Hortensia. It's getting late!

ESPERANZA: I'll go with you and ask about a job.

MODESTA: What?
Who will stay with Carlitos?

HORTENSIA: We cannot ask Isabel to miss school.

ESPERANZA: I know. I know.

MODESTA: There are no jobs open.

ESPERANZA: What shall I do?

MODESTA: About what?

ESPERANZA: I need to work! I must save money and go get my *mamá* and bring her here or something terrible will happen. I know it!

HORTENSIA: We can't talk now. We'll talk later. We help each other. We'll think of something!

(The bell rings.)

MODESTA: Wait! *(She undoes her apron and her bandana and gives them to* ESPERANZA.*)* You! Take my job for awhile.

ESPERANZA: No. Not your job.

MODESTA: The bosses won't know. We all look alike to them!

ESPERANZA: But the money?

MODESTA: Alfonso works. We have enough for now.

ESPERANZA: Enough? You have nothing!

MODESTA: If I had been rich, it might seem like we have nothing. But for us, it is enough to live on.

ESPERANZA: You would do that for me?

MODESTA: I do this for me and for Carlitos.

ESPERANZA: I know you miss him all day. But you are making a sacrifice. For me.

MODESTA: That too.

ESPERANZA: But why?

MODESTA: I am sick of seeing people who live without hope!

ESPERANZA: But...

MODESTA: No but. Go!

ESPERANZA: How can I ever thank you?

MODESTA: Work hard. Bring your mother soon.

*(*ESPERANZA *and* MODESTA *embrace.)*

(End of Scene Three)

Scene Four

(On one side, in the shed, a line of women including Hortensia *are cutting up potatoes at a long table. Every two workers share two large baskets. Some pieces are thrown into one basket, the leftovers into the other basket. Field workers enter now and then bringing empty baskets and removing the full ones. Once in a while one of the women grabs a broom and sweeps the floor clean. The women wear sweaters and gloves, bandanas and big aprons.)*

(To enter the shed, workers must pass through a gauntlet of strikers. Marta *is among them. The strikers chanting.)*

The Crowd: *(Chanting)* Huelga, Huelga
Don't let our children starve!
Unite with us *compadres!*
Huelga, huelga. Strike, strike
We won't starve without a fight!

(A few strikers have loudspeakers and they yell over the chanting:
"Join us compadres,"
"Strike now. Help us feed our children"
As people pass the picket line, the strikers and the workers yell back and forth.)

The Strikers: Cowards! Traitors!

Workers: Leave us alone!
Our children are hungry too. We need to work. I must support my mother. I came here to work. You lazy bums!

*(*Esperanza *fights through the strikers, someone grabs her bandana which she grabs back. She joins* Hortensia *in the shed. The strikers move offstage still chanting and yelling and we are in the shed.)*

Woman Worker I: All that shouting drives me crazy!

Woman Worker II: The strikers are making it worse.

Woman Worker III: How could things get worse?

Women: Shhhhh.

Esperanza: *(To* Hortensia*)* What do I do?

Hortensia: Just do as I do. First cut the potato into pieces.

Woman Worker I: *(Making a little dance out of

it)* Cut potatoes into pieces.

HORTENSIA: Cut around the eyes.

WOMAN WORKER II: *(Doing the same)* Cut around the eyes.

ESPERANZA: *(Almost dropping hers)* Potatoes have eyes?

HORTENSIA: *(Lifting and showing her)* This is a potato eye.

ESPERANZA: Oh. *(General laughter)*

HORTENSIA: Drop this part in this basket. The men will come to take them away.

WOMEN: Ay men! *(Some laughter)*

HORTENSIA: They plant the eyes in the field. And new potatoes grow from them.

ESPERANZA: So that's where potatoes come from!

(The WOMEN, along with HORTENSIA and ESPERANZA continue their task, some making a rhythmic song.)

EVERYONE: First cut the potato into pieces. Cut around the eye...etc...

(All of a sudden there is silence.)

WOMAN WORKER I: Do you hear that?

HORTENSIA: What? What do you hear?

WOMAN WORKER I: The silence.

WOMEN: *Ay si.*

(They are all quiet for a moment. Then we hear sirens and buses and yelling!)

WOMAN WORKER III: Oh my God! *La Migra!*

ESPERANZA: What?

HORTENSIA: Immigration. It's a sweep!

WOMAN WORKER II: *(Desperately looking for a place to hide)* My mother is sick! They can't take me!

HORTENSIA: *Calmate, m'hija.* They won't take you. You're a worker. You have a job.

WOMAN WORKER II: *Ay dios!* I have no one to take care of her.

ESPERANZA: Will they send us back?

HORTENSIA: Keep working. They're not here for us. The growers need the workers.
That's why we have guards.

WOMAN WORKER I: You look Mexican. Boom boom—on the bus.

(Two male workers enter, carrying a very heavy basket. They put it in the back of the shed with other baskets and leave. An immigration agent with gun drawn comes in and looks around. Walks between each worker and looks her in the eye.)

AGENT: Has anyone come in here?

WOMAN WORKER I: No. Only us.

HORTENSIA: Can't you see, we're just working?!

WOMAN WORKER I: Put your gun away.

HORTENSIA: *Sin verguenza!* You don't have to scare us!

WOMAN WORKER I: We have mouths to feed.

HORTENSIA: We don't want any trouble.

AGENT: A girl was running this way. Did you see her?

(Guard II walks among them. As he passes, each one says "no" in turn. ESPERANZA *has trouble looking up.)*

AGENT: If any of you hide a striker—we'll pack you on a bus and send you back to Mexico. Just like them! Do you hear?

WOMEN: Yes.

WOMAN WORKER I: Basket!

ESPERANZA: I'll get it.

*(*ESPERANZA *opens one basket.* MARTA *is inside)*

MARTA: Shhhhhhhhh.

*(*ESPERANZA *says nothing and returns to the line of workers.)*

WOMAN WORKER III: Did you forget my basket, Cinderella?

ESPERANZA: Yes. Yes. I forgot! *(She goes back to the baskets.)*

*(*ESPERANZA *takes off her apron and quickly stuffs it into the basket* MARTA *is in and brings another basket to* WOMAN WORKER III. *Then she gets the broom to sweep. She goes to the basket* MARTA *is in.)*

ESPERANZA: *(She whispers.)* Marta?!

MARTA: Yes?

ESPERANZA: When we leave, leave with us. Put on the apron and carry some potatoes so you look like a worker.

MARTA: You mean it?

ESPERANZA: Yes.

MARTA: You'll help me?

ESPERANZA: Yes.

MARTA: Thank you.

(ESPERANZA *stops sweeping and returns to* HORTENSIA.)

AGENT: The strikers aren't your friends, you know. They aren't protecting you.
I hear they put glass among the potatoes so you cut your hands. I hear they put rattlesnakes in some of your work baskets to slow you down. Is that true?

(*No one answers. They all work.* AGENT *continues to check the baskets.*)

AGENT: Has anyone checked those for snakes or rats?

(*No one answers. Frightened,* ESPERANZA *looks back at the baskets where* MARTA *is hiding.*)

AGENT: (*To* ESPERANZA) You like that basket?

ESPERANZA: No.

AGENT: I like those baskets. (*He lifts the top of the basket where* MARTA *is hiding.*) Well, well, well...these strikers put snakes everywhere!

(MARTA *scrambles out and tries to run. The* AGENT *catches her.*)

AGENT: Gotcha!

MARTA: Let me go. I'm an American citizen. It's a free country.

AGENT: (*As he drags her out*) Yes, you're free to leave if you don't like it here.

MARTA: I'm American!

AGENT: Your papers?

MARTA: I don't need papers. I'm a citizen.

AGENT: Not with that face! You wanna make trouble? Make trouble in Mexico! Go back where you belong!

MARTA: (*Struggle*) I belong here. I was born here!

(*The* AGENT *wrestles* MARTA *out.*)

MARTA: *Huelga!* Strike! Unite so our people can eat!

(*They exit struggling.*)

MARTA: *Venceremos!*

(HORTENSIA *lets out a wail.*)

ESPERANZA: Oh no! No!

WOMAN WORKER I: Hush.

WOMAN WORKER II: Keep working.

ESPERANZA: I was afraid for her. I couldn't help looking! I'm sorry.

HORTENSIA: It's not fair. She was born here. She knows no one in Mexico.

WOMAN WORKER II: Keep working!

WOMAN WORKER I: Unite. *Unidos venceremos!*

WOMAN WORKER II: Shut up or we'll all be on that bus!

ESPERANZA: I'm sorry.

(End of Scene Four)

Scene Five

(The fiesta; a fiesta at the camp is just beginning. Women carry plates of food. Men are drinking. The MARIACHIS are there too. One is dressed in full Mariachi regalia, one is in work clothes but wears his sombrero, the other has on his Mariachi trousers, a cowboy hat and a Brooklyn Dodgers shirt which he shows off to his buddies and takes an umpire's stance calling an "out" on someone sliding into home plate. When approached by the others he keeps saying..."Yerrrrrr out".)

(The Okie family we saw at the border reappears, looking hungrily at all the food. Everyone ignores them until they start to play and sing and pass the hat. The little BOY dances. A circle forms around then. People clapping.)

(Stage left...ESPERANZA is stuffing a jar full of bills. She holds her doll and talks to her.)

ESPERANZA: Ten more dollars. Ten more dollars—that's four more weeks!

ISABEL: Come to the dance!

ESPERANZA: Isabel!

ISABEL: Ooooooo. Look at all the money. You're rich again!

ESPERANZA: Shhhhh. I don't want the whole world to know. This is money to bring my mother! Now *cállate!*

ISABEL: Then *ven.* Come dance. Your doll wants to go. I can tell. *(To the doll)* "Hello *chiquitita bonita.* Do you know how to dance?"
Have you given her a name yet?

ESPERANZA: Not yet.

ISABEL: Call her Reina! I might be a reina soon too. The best girl student in third grade is chosen every year to be Queen of the May.
And guess what?

ESPERANZA: You're going to be Queen of the May?

ISABEL: My teacher said I'm the best student—girls and boys!
So, I'm going to pray every day.

ESPERANZA: That's good. But I think other girls will be praying too!

ISABEL: I'll pray hardest! I want so much to be queen. I want to wear a new dress and hold the Maypole so everyone can dance around me holding colored ribbons. Then there will be three *"reinas"* You, *chiquitita* and me! Hooray!
Aren't you going to the dance?

ESPERANZA: No.

ISABEL: I am. Can I take your doll?

ESPERANZA: NO!

(ISABEL *looks out of the room at the fiesta. The little Okie* BOY *starts to dance and his parents sing.* HORTENSIA *enters.*)

ISABEL: Oooo—look the Okie family's here.

HORTENSIA: Now what's this "Okie"? I hear all the time.

ISABEL: "Okie" is short for Oklahoma. It's a state. There was no rain and all the land blew away in the wind—so the Okies had to come here like us. Only, they're lucky. They have hot water and they're going to have a swimming pool. They can use it everyday, but we can only use it on Fridays.

HORTENSIA: And why only Fridays?

ISABEL: Because they clean the pool right after we swim!

ESPERANZA: Why?! Do they think we're dirtier than other people?

ISABEL: I don't know.
Look! Come on. The Okie boy is dancing!

ESPERANZA: You go ahead.

ISABEL: Okey-dokey. (*She skips out and joins the crowd watching the Okies.*)

HORTENSIA: Go dance.

ESPERANZA: No.

HORTENSIA: Why not?

ESPERANZA: I can't face anyone. Not after Marta! I gave her to La Migra!

HORTENSIA: No one blames you. You didn't mean to.

ESPERANZA: I blame myself. I didn't know how bad things could be.

(The crowd is clapping. The MARIACHIS *are playing along with the family—once in a while joining in a refrain. Everyone is happy.* ISABEL *watches and then begins to dance with the little* BOY. *Soon other people begin to dance.)*

*(*MIGUEL *enters, covered in mud, intent on going straight to his cabin. He catches sight of* ISABEL *and grabs her by the arm and hauls her into the bedroom.)*

MIGUEL: Ven acá! Caray!
What do you think you're doing?

ISABEL: What?

MIGUEL: Making a spectacle of yourself with that...that Okie!!

ISABEL: He's just a boy dancing!

MIGUEL: Well you can't dance with him!

ESPERANZA: Miguel!

MIGUEL: We're not friends with Okies.

ISABEL: *(Getting loose)* He can be my friend.

MIGUEL: Okies are bad news for us!
A group of men showed up from Oklahoma. They said they would work for half the money and the railroad hired all of them! Some of them never even worked on a motor before. My boss said he wouldn't need me any more! He was going to train the Okies.

ESPERANZA: Just because some Okies made you mad- it isn't all the Okies fault!
Isabel You go dance with whom you want!

*(*ISABEL *goes back to the dance, but only watches.)*

ESPERANZA: How did you get so dirty?

MIGUEL: My boss said I could dig ditches and lay tracks if I wanted.

ESPERANZA: And what did you do?

MIGUEL: Can't you tell from my clothes? I dug ditches!

ESPERANZA: Miguel—how could you agree to such a thing?!

MIGUEL: What would you have me do? Walk away? With no paycheck? Do you want us to starve?

ESPERANZA: Why didn't your boss tell the others to dig ditches!

MIGUEL: Why do you think?

ESPERANZA: Because you're Mexican?
Did you say anything?

MIGUEL: What would be the use of that? Eh?

ESPERANZA: So you did nothing?

MIGUEL: I worked.
Does that offend you?

ESPERANZA: How dare you say that to me.

MIGUEL: Then what? Maybe I should go up north to Oregon to work, so seeing me wouldn't offend you!

ESPERANZA: Stay here. Stand up for yourself!

MIGUEL: I'll do what I want.
What's the matter with you?

ESPERANZA: The matter with me?
You wanted to come to the United States. So here we are. And what? Is this the better life you left Mexico for? Is it? Nothing is better here. Nothing is right! You can't work on engines because you're Mexican. We go to work through angry crowds of our own people who are so poor they throw rocks at us or they're kidnapped and thrown from a bus into Mexico. White camps get indoor toilets and hot water and swimming pools but not us! Why is that, Miguel? Why not us? Is it because we're Mexicans and we'll always be Mexicans no matter how long we live here or how hard we work? Tell me, is this life really better for you than life in Mexico?

MIGUEL: Yes. It is. In Mexico, I was a second class citizen. A peasant. I could never change that! I was born on the wrong side of a river—do you remember, *reina*? At least here I have a chance, however small, to become more than what I was. You obviously can never understand this because you were on the right side of the river. You never lived without hope!

ESPERANZA: How can you say that now? I've lost everything. Every single thing that meant anything to me—my *papá*, my friends, my land, my education and all I was meant to be. I'm not even thirteen! I need my mother here—but for all I know I may never see her again!
I think it's you who doesn't understand. You crossed the river, but you're still a second class citizen. Why? Because you act like one. You let the bosses take advantage of you. They won't give Mexicans a chance. Why don't you go to your bosses and confront them? Why don't you speak up for yourself and your talents and your people?
Be a man!

MIGUEL: *(Grabs the doll and shoves it at her)* Why don't you go play with dolls!

ESPERANZA: Look at yourself. You still believe you're a peasant! *(She exits and goes over to* ISABEL *to watch the people dancing.)*

MIGUEL: And you still think you're a queen! *(He takes* ESPERANZA's *doll and money drops out. He stuffs it in his pocket and exits.)*

(End of Scene Five)

Scene Six

(The roses are blooming in their cans and all over the stage. ESPERANZA *and* HORTENSIA *are pruning and watering them.* ESPERANZA's *doll sits at the feet of the Madonna. Two* MARIACHIS *are playing. The third will enter as the* MAILMAN.*)*

MAILMAN: Mail! Mail! *Paquetes y correo!* Rafael Gomez de Ochoa
Angel Romano Perez
Natalia Valdes Flores

(A woman runs up to get her letter.)

MAILMAN: *Cartas de tus amores!*

(She slaps MAILMAN *playfully and he laughs.)*

MAILMAN: Adolfo Hernandez
Inocencia Zavala. *(He exits still calling names.)*
Maria Andrea Medina
Here's your *medecina. (Sees* ESPERANZA*)* Not for you little one!
Mail! Mail!
Paquetes y correo.

ESPERANZA: Not a word from my *mama*! I've been away from her for so long! I don't think she will ever come. And now—I have no money. It will take me months to save again. Maybe I'll never see my *mamá* again! Miguel has spoiled everything! I almost hate these roses—because Miguel brought them! Every day they remind me that Miguel is a thief, a *buitre* just like my Tio Luis.

HORTENSIA: I understand how you feel about Miguel. I am very ashamed. But *que culpa tienen las rosas*? How can you hate roses? Look at them. How they've opened and bloomed even ripped from Mexican soil like us.

ESPERANZA: I don't really hate them and I don't really hate Miguel. Part of what he did is my fault. I got angry and called him a "peasant" and then he left.

HORTENSIA: So you hurt his pride and he left to mend it. He will come back soon. He's not one to stay away from his family for long. I'm sure he will bring you back your money.

ESPERANZA: *(Picking up a can)* I think these roses are getting too big for the cans. Will they die?

HORTENSIA: If we don't plant them in the ground here so they put down roots, they'll die. They need the land to breathe, to live, to grow—even this strange land where no one speaks their language or knows their heart. If the roses don't make their home in this soil, they will die. Like us. We have no choice. We are not going to die, so we will also put our roots down here.

(ESPERANZA *throws herself to the ground and lies still.*)

HORTENSIA: Esperanza! Anza! What are you doing?

ESPERANZA: Listening.

MODESTA: For what?

ESPERANZA: For a heartbeat. For a breath. Anything! *(She gets back up.)* I hear nothing. Nothing. This land will never speak to me.
Maybe, if I never open my eyes again, I will fall all the way back to Mexico.

(ISABEL *rushes in with her school books and throws them on the ground.*)

ISABEL: It's not fair! It's not fair.
I didn't win Queen of the May. I had the best grades but the teacher said she chose on more than just grades! The Queen has to be blond!

ALFONSO: I'm sorry. I'm sorry *mi amorcita*. They didn't choose you. Well, you will always be my queen! Who cares about Queen of the May.

ISABEL: I care! I tried so hard!

ESPERANZA: *Ay* Isabel, come here. *(She hugs her.)* You would have made a beautiful May Queen—but that lasts only one day. A day goes by fast and then it's over.

ISABEL: But I prayed and prayed and prayed to be Queen of the May!

ESPERANZA: I know you did, but Isabelita, do you know what I think?

ISABEL: What?

ESPERANZA: I think Our Lady knew things you didn't know.
I think Our Lady was very wise in not granting your prayers.

ISABEL: What do you mean?

ESPERANZA: She wanted you to have something that would last more than one day.

ISABEL: Like what?

ESPERANZA: Hmmmmmm. *(Giving her the doll)* Like this. To keep as your own.

ISABEL: Ohh...no Esperanza. Your *papá* gave this to you.

ESPERANZA: Do you think my *papá* would want her buried inside a valise all the time with no one playing with her? Look at her—she'd be too lonely. And look at me—I'm almost thirteen. I'm much too old for dolls. You would be doing me and my *papá* a favor if you would love her.

ISABEL: Really?

ESPERANZA: Yes. And you know what else?

ISABEL: What?

ESPERANZA: I think you should take her to school and show all your friends. I'm sure that not even the Queen of the May has a doll as beautiful as this!

(ISABEL *takes the doll and jumps up and down.*)

ISABEL: Thank you. Thank you.
I'll call her "Reina"
I think my heart is dancing! *(She dances with the doll and stops suddenly.)*
Oh no!

ESPERANZA: What's the matter?

ISABEL: What will your *mamá* say?

(MIGUEL *enters.*)

MIGUEL: I think her *mamá* would say she's very, very proud of her daughter.

RAMONA: Esperanza!

ESPERANZA: Mamá! Mamá! Is it you? *De veras?*

(They rush to embrace each other.)

RAMONA: *M'hija. Aquí estoy.* I'm here. I'm here. How I missed you!

ESPERANZA: Mamá!

RAMONA: Hortensia!

HORTENSIA: Doña!

(HORTENSIA *and* RAMONA *embrace.*)

RAMONA: You must call me "Ramona" now. A thousand thanks can never repay you for taking in my daughter!

ESPERANZA: *(To* MIGUEL*)* But how…?

MIGUEL: I felt you were right. Marta was right. Our lives will not get better until we take action ourselves. So I took my action. I snuck to the convent in Aguascalientes. Your *tio* still had his men at the train station so your mother dressed as a nun, and we took the train back. *Punto.*

ISABEL: This is your mother?

ESPERANZA: This is my mother! Mamá, this is our cousin, Isabel and her *papá* Alfonso.

ISABEL: You came from a convent? You don't look like a nun!

RAMONA: Thank you, Isabel. I think you and I are going to be good friends. *(To* ESPERANZA*)* Esperanza, look at you! How you've grown! And look at all these roses. So sweet. So beautiful.

ESPERANZA: Miguel brought them from our garden.

RAMONA: Our garden! Our beautiful garden! Here?! God bless you, Miguel.

ESPERANZA: But the roots have outgrown their little pots They may not last much longer.

RAMONA: Then we must transplant them. Today.

ESPERANZA: Do you think they'll grow here? The soil's not the same.

RAMONA: It's not the same, but it looks very rich. Why don't we plant them and see?

(They all kneel and start to dig. The MARIACHIS *enter to sing: Adios—Bienvenida [Good Bye—Hello].)*

MARIACHI 1: If you look up at the sky
What do you see?
The same slivered moon
That always shined on me
The same silver clouds The same whirling stars.
Who would think that all below
Is so changed by where we are?

Adios, adios
Adios, adios
My Love
How sad was my goodbye
Adios, adios
Adios, adios
My Love
Your death now makes me cry.

(The next verse interrupts this one with a new vision...or this first verse can be sung earlier in the play with the next verse as the only closing verse.)

MARIACHI 2: But look around
The earth smells sweet
The birds still fly Mothers with their girls
Delight.

The world turns
The sun still warms
Seedlings stretch and are reborn
How beautiful this morning comes
Like wanderers we're welcomed home

MARIACHI 3: *Bienvenido, bienvenidas*
Con gusto y placer
Te arrimas.

Bienvenidos, bienvenidas
Welcome, welcome home
To see us.

END OF PLAY

ROMOLA & NIJINSKY

Deux Mariages

ROMOLA & NIJINSKY was first produced on 20 April 2003 by Primary Stages (Casey Childs, Executive Producer; Andrew Leynse, Artistic Director). The cast and creative contributor were:

ROMOLA	Kelly Hutchinson
NIJINSKY	David Barlow
BARON	Allen Fitzpatrick
EMILIA & ANNA	Janet Zarish
DIAGHELIFF/VASSILY	Daniel Oreskes
THE MAN WITH THE PIPE	John McAdams
DANCERS	Michelle Lookadoo, Laura Martin, & Matt Rivera
Director	David Levine
Choreography	Robert La Fosse
Set design	Michael Byrnes
Costume design	Claudia Stephens
Lighting design	Lao-Chi Chu
Sound design	Jane Shaw
Original composition	Brendan Connelly
Prop design	Laurie Marvald
Production stage manager	Erika Timperman
Assistant stage manager	Diane M Ballering
Production manager	Lester P Grant
Production consultant	Fran Kirmser
Assistant directors	Kathryn Moroney & Loe Mackler
Casting	Stephanie Klapper
Press representative	Jeffrey Richards Associates

Special funding for the production was provided by The Peter Jay Sharp Foundation and The Russell Fellowship for Playwrights.

CHARACTERS & SETTING

ROMOLA DE PULSKY, *twenty, dancer in the Corps de Ballet of the Ballets Russes*
VASLAV NIJINSKY, *twenty-one, soloist and star of the Ballet Russes*
BARON DIMITRI DE GUNSBOURG, *forty-five, Russian aristocrat, major backer and Acting-Director of the Ballets Russes on tour*
EMILIA MARKUS, *forty-five, great Hungarian classical actress and* ROMOLA's *mother*
SERGEI DIAGHELIFF, *forty-five, creator and Director of the Ballets Russes, formerly* NIJINSKY's *lover and mentor.*
ANNA, *forty,* ROMOLA's *companion/attendant*
VASSILY, *sixty,* DIAGHELIFF's *valet passed on to* NIJINSKY
THE MAN WITH THE PIPE (RUPERT), *anywhere from thirty to sixty. English passenger, polymorphos, perverse*

Three DANCERS, *two women and one man*

The DANCERS *play all minor roles including, the ship's captain, maids, waiters, prostitutes, the priest and couples promenading on deck etc. regardless of gender. The* DANCERS *should preferably be ballet dancers and do some of their movements on point. There are several full dance numbers as indicated in the script and at times the dancers do have minimal lines to say. However—despite the particular character they may portray in any given moment—they should first and foremost be seen as dancers portraying a role, i.e. they should walk like dancers, should feel free to do dance steps as they move about and their costumes might be fitted rather obviously over their basic dance outfits and shoes. Since these dancers are mischievous and sometimes worse—their basic costume should reflect this. Please use the dancers to augment, mirror, introduce or bridge action on stage although with the caveat that they do not either crowd or intrude upon the ongoing action of the play or the intimacy of any scenes.*

We never see NIJINSKY *dance.*

Variously—a ballroom in Saint Moritz, Switzerland on January 19, 1919; aboard the S S Avon during the month of August 1913; a church in Buenos Aires on September 10, 1913. Sets are optional.

ACT ONE

PROLOGUE

(January 19, 1919. A private home. Saint Moritz, Switzerland. A night sky. Instead of stars we gradually realize there are a variety of eyes overhead: some blinking, some staring, some human and others of animals. NIJINSKY *is in a circle of light. He is wearing practical clothes. Far upstage right in another spot of light is a dancer dressed as* NIJINSKY *doing Petrouschka. He dances. At some point during* NIJINSKY's *speech, he turns and turns and turns and turns and turns and disappears.)*

(Some characters enter with chairs facing the audience—as if the audience is the performance. ROMOLA *enters beautifully, elegantly dressed with her mother,* EMILIA. DIAGHELIFF *enters in tails. They sit. We hear the opening of* Petrouschka.*)*

*(*ROMOLA *bends toward* EMILIA *and whispers. Her voice, however, is projected over the music and dancing.)*

ROMOLA: This is the greatest role, ma mere, exquisite. Petrouschka dies, of course.
For love, what else is there? Watch him, how he suffers, how he extends with a trembling arm his agony and sadness to the only people who understand him—the gray common crowd of Russia. Is it not extraordinary how he seems to be made of wood and yet executes the most difficult steps? Look at those pirouettes and *toures en l'air*. Perfect, perfect, but always in character. And you will see the suffering of this doll, Petrouschka. In his last breath, even, Petrouschka's heart is filled with love for the ballerina. He sends her his last tragic kiss. See how he presses the palm of his hand to his pale lips and trembling, jerking...see...see how he does it! He extends his arm toward the vastness of space. Oh, yes. *(She stands.)* Bravo, bravissimo.

(Everyone stands and claps as the music does not stop, but repeats.)

ROMOLA: But what's wrong?

EMILIA: He is still dancing!

DIAGHELIFF: Stop, Vatza!

ROMOLA: Oh, Vaslav, stop!

(End of Prologue)

Scene One

(It is August 1913. We are on the S S Avon *heading to South America. Piquant music. The scene begins with a 2:32 minute dance which establishes being aboard ship. First there is a "pas de trois" with the Captain and two passengers who arrive. Tickets are requested and checked, boxes carried etc. other passengers arrive cross, meet and acknowledge each other or not. The dancers wave to people on shore. Point out things of interest, jostling each other for a better view and competing for the captain's attention. The dancers are always dancing—very mannered, very turn of the century ballet—while the other passengers are walking naturally, promenading on deck in character. The* BARON, *organizing other people, the man with the pipe flirting with anything that moves—but especially the* BARON *and* ANNA *when the* BARON *isn't looking.* ROMOLA *and* ANNA *enter.)*

ROMOLA: Of course he's extreme Anna. He's a genius and he's Russian!

(One of the dancers sees something in the sky and drops to her knees and crosses herself. She points it out to the other dancer who crosses herself many times.)

ANNA: Barbarians! They're all mad if you ask me. Impossibly superstitious. My God if a crow flies overhead—they're all on their knees crossing themselves.

(The Englishman smoking a pipe walks by.)

ANNA: I think I will learn to smoke a pipe.

ROMOLA: I can't believe you like that Englishman. He's so common!

ANNA: Shhhhhhh.

ROMOLA: He doesn't understand Hungarian, Anna. No one understands Hungarian.
  Now come over here. Look at the ocean. It's endless.

ANNA: It moves too much

ROMOLA: It's lovely. I hope Buenos Aires will have beaches like they do in Italy—with all those dark men following us whispering obscenities.

ANNA: I'm going to follow my Englishman.

ROMOLA: What? You?

ANNA: Yes. Romola. I have decided to take advantage of this voyage. I shall follow my heart for once. I may be an old maid—but I needn't have an unscathed hymen as well!

(NIJINSKY *enters. He is followed by* VASSILY *holding a towel and watering can.* NIJINSKY *is stopped by admirers.* VASSILY *takes the moment to wipe away* NIJINSKY's *perspiration.*)

ROMOLA: Anna!
You can't go.

ANNA: Yes I can.

ROMOLA: No. *Le Petit.*

ANNA: Please!

ROMOLA: You can't leave me now. I need you.
Thank you Divine Child for allowing me to live in this century and to have seen Nijinsky dance!
How do I look?

ANNA: Awful.

ROMOLA: Is he looking at me? (*She laughs loudly, posing.*)

ANNA: No.

ROMOLA: Wait!

(ROMOLA *takes out a cigarette.* ANNA *reluctantly lights it.*)

ANNA: Those Turkish things. Oh that should make a wonderful impression. Now we'll both smell like camel dung. Blow the smoke the other way.

ROMOLA: Is he watching yet?

ANNA: No.

ROMOLA: What's he doing?

ANNA: He's stopped practicing and Vassily is wiping his armpits.

ROMOLA: I must be mad—I want to kiss him there. Yes. And in that cleft under his lower lip where perhaps no one has ever kissed him before.

(ROMOLA *blows out a plume of smoke and* VASSILY *approaches angrily.*)

VASSILY: Away! Away! Go! Very bad!

ROMOLA: What did he say? He speaks French like a barking dog.

ANNA: He wants us to leave.

ROMOLA: Yes Vassily. All right.

(ROMOLA *makes a great show of putting out her cigarette.* VASSILY *turns to leave and she says very loudly.*)

ROMOLA: Vassily's such a little old lady with his little towel and watering can. He probably accompanies Vaslav to the loo and wipes his bottom.

ANNA: Hush!

ROMOLA: They don't understand Hungarian.

ANNA: Well don't say their names. They understand that!

ROMOLA: *(Walking by* NIJINSKY *who still doesn't glace her way.)* How rude. He hasn't given me a glance. I can't stand it. You'd think he never saw me before. But he was so attentive in Budapest when he mistook me for the *prima ballerina* of the Hungarian Opera. I allowed him to kiss my hand— even though he looked like some poor Japanese student with that Tartar face and ill-fitting clothes. But—oh—he moved like a tiger—so soft and fierce. Now he's impossible! I'll show him I can ignore him too. *(She laughs.)* Of course—first he has to notice me ignoring him! Oh please, Miraculous Jesus of Prague, Divine Child—be with me every minute. Let me move like a feather, like an angel, like a drum. I know the only way to his heart is through the dance!

(ROMOLA *drags* ANNA *off.* VASSILY *drapes a towel around* NIJINSKY's *shoulders as they exit, but one of the* DANCERS *snatches it and smells it and shares it with the other. They exit. We hear the slow rise and fall of the ocean against the ship. A couple walks by. The woman is angry and precedes the man with a pipe who is pleading with her. They exit. The lights darken. The* BARON *enters wearing a white linen suit, humming parts of the firebird. He stops to conduct when he comes to an especially lively passage. He wraps a bright shawl around his waist as he continues on to* NIJINSKY's *cabin.)*

(End of Scene One)

Scene Two

(NIJINSKY *is sitting on the massage table as the masseur gathers up his things. The masseur has an interesting "tic". When the masseur's back is turned,* NIJINSKY *studies his movements and tries to reproduce them. There is a knock on the door.)*

BARON: Vasla, Vaslav, may I come in? It is I, Dimitri.

NIJINSKY: What's the matter?

BARON: I can't bear to be alone.

NIJINSKY: It's only an hour to dinner.

BARON: I know, I know.

(*The masseur opens the door and the* BARON *enters. The masseur gives a slight bow and a dance step and leaves. The* BARON *notices* NIJINSKY *doing the imitation.)*

BARON: What is it? What's wrong? Vaslav, are you having a fit? Oh, I see you're doing one of your studies. Well you do look just like that man, but why would you want to? You should do me? Oh no, that would be too pathetic. But tell me, how do I look? I tried this sash for a bit of color and dash, as we are going to South America. *Olé.* Oh, I can just imagine what your dear Sergei would say, "Dimitri, you look like an aging whore." Odd, I don't miss him, but I'm always quoting him. How indelicate. Personally, I think this separation from Sergei will do you wonders, not that I don't understand your relationship. I had one myself, very romantic, rose petals on the bed, that sort of thing. But, I knew it was doomed. He would always arrive from Kiev with this very small valise. I'd take one look at that very small valise and think, "He's already planning to leave". I felt deserted as soon as he arrived.

NIJINSKY: Please don't talk about love, Dimitri.

BARON: Yes, of course. Passion is nothing but an inferno. Except for dance, of course.

NIJINSKY: Of course.

BARON: Ah, dance. You are so brilliant!

NIJINSKY: You are so transparent. What is it you want, Dimitri?

BARON: I think it's time you rethought your relationship with Diagheliff. I know how deathly tired you are of all his intrigue. Sergei runs the Ballets Russes like a Caliph's court, full of favorites and concubines.

NIJINSKY: Yes.

BARON: Yes well...I have a thought— You and I should start a small company. We could achieve some interesting results, don't you think? No. No. No. Don't answer me now. Think about it. In the meantime, let's play. I have it in mind to introduce you to someone who is quite rich and quite mad for you.

NIJINSKY: I'm not interested. Thank you, Baron.

BARON: Come. Come. The cure for disenchantment is love. If you're interested in girls, there's a beautiful girl on board I think you should meet. She's taken every opportunity to drape herself in front of you. You must have noticed.

NIJINSKY: The blue-eyed girl?

BARON: Yes, yes. That's her.

NIJINSKY: Is she a dancer?

BARON: In the *corps de ballet*, I believe.

NIJINSKY: But the *corps de ballet* is in second class and this girl has a cabin near mine.

BARON: Oh, she's very rich. Her mother is a great classical actress, the premier actress of Hungary, actually. Some say she is as great as Bernhardt. *(Whispering)* She was the seventh child of a button manufacturer.

NIJINSKY: The blue-eyed girl?

BARON: No, her mother. But she became a great actress and married de Pulsky, an aristocrat, which in turn made her very wealthy, which in turn made Romola, that is the blue-eyed girl, a beneficiary of the money. What I am trying to say is, she has money and you should meet her.

NIJINSKY: Does she dance well?

BARON: I can't say. I've never seen her dance. She's only just joined the company for this tour.

NIJINSKY: I could never be interested in any girl who wasn't a beautiful dancer.

BARON: Oh for heaven's sakes—why limit yourself to *prima ballerinas*? You should meet this girl. She's quite pretty and has eyes like sapphires. Perhaps she is a good dancer. Who knows? I will introduce you.

NIJINSKY: No need.

BARON: But why?

NIJINSKY: We've already met.

BARON: I see.

NIJINSKY: Yes.

BARON: Sooo...you hate her.

NIJINSKY: Oh no.

BARON: But you never greet her and she never greets you.

NIJINSKY: I make a display of not noticing her.

BARON: For God's sakes why? She's from a very good family.

NIJINSKY: I enjoy provoking her to flirt. It's always a pleasure to watch someone do what they do best. I'm perfectly happy Baron, to observe love like a beautiful painting of a landscape. It's enchanting and I don't have to inhabit it!

BARON: Pity.

NIJINSKY: You seem awfully determined that we should meet. And why is that, Dimitri? Do you want her to come between me and Sergei Pavlovitch? Will she give her riches to our new company?

BARON: No, I would never presume...

NIJINSKY: I am the Ballets Russes. I would never desert her.

BARON: What if she deserts you?

NIJINSKY: What do you mean? Why do you say that?

BARON: Sergei doesn't really appreciate your choreography the way he should. I adored *Sacre* and *Jeux*—although I admit not many others did. And he wasn't very fond of *L'Apres Midi*.

NIJINSKY: Why? What have you heard?

BARON: Actually I heard that he refuses to give *Faune* in Paris. He said: "It's not a ballet. I'd sooner dismiss the company before I give it again!" But then—perhaps it's all gossip. You know what a shallow bitch I am.

NIJINSKY: So shallow, but so clever. Well! I leave you to your motives and ask you to take me on deck and show me how to smoke a pipe like a proper Englishman.

BARON: A pipe? What makes you think I know...? Oh... Ohhhh. Yes, oh, so you saw me with that lovely gentleman. He's quite impressive and he knows everything about Hindu ruins. He's been hunting with a minor *maharajah*. He's wild about animals, so sensitive. He told me he would give his soul if, just once, he could watch an elephant drink. He's offered to take me on safari through the jungles of the Amazon—but I can't possibly go. Suppose the relationship is brief? Safari clothes are so costly and it would be a perfect waste of money to have them made if the relationship were brief. I mean, where else could I use them? Certainly not with my wife.

(End of Scene Two)

Scene Three

(ROMOLA and ANNA are sitting on deck chairs. ROMOLA is daydreaming with a book in her lap and ANNA is carefully putting on lotion. The MAN WITH THE PIPE walks by. He greets both ladies but he is eyeing ANNA.)

MAN WITH THE PIPE: Good day, *mademoiselles*. Lovely morning.

ANNA: A fine day to you, too, *Monsieur*.

(Their eyes linger.)

MAN WITH THE PIPE: This equatorial sun is terribly hot, don't you think?

ANNA: Have we crossed the equator, then?

MAN WITH THE PIPE: No. Tonight. Is this your first time?

ANNA: First time...?

MAN WITH THE PIPE: Crossing.

ANNA: Oh, yes, and yours?

MAN WITH THE PIPE: My third.

ANNA: Oh.

MAN WITH THE PIPE: Yes, they'll give you little silk flags of all the nations that touch the equator.

(The BARON *and* NIJINSKY *are promenading on the deck. They walk by and the* BARON *gives the* MAN WITH THE PIPE *a flirtatious look. The* MAN WITH THE PIPE *turns his back coldly and obviously.)*

MAN WITH THE PIPE: Yes...well, ladies, enjoy your morning. *(He continues to walk.)*

ROMOLA: Was that him?

ANNA: Who?

ROMOLA: Please. I saw that look pass between you. If you ask me, he was altogether too familiar.

ANNA: Yes, I'll go tell him at once. *(She gets up.)*

ROMOLA: I can't believe you're going to follow him?

ANNA: I have no time to lose.

ROMOLA: But what do you know about him?

ANNA: He's shown interest in me. He's English and he smokes a pipe. I'll tell you more about him when I get back. Ta!

ROMOLA: Go! Leave me alone then, you hussy!

*(*ANNA *exits in the direction of the man.* ROMOLA *takes up a book. Two women prostitutes walk by in deep discussion.)*

WOMAN 2: Pickles and vodka?

WOMAN 1: But he has an estate.

WOMAN 2: I suppose you can't resist.

WOMAN 1: I don't know. The village is backward, the peasants are drunk, and the roads are impassable.

(The women sit. ROMOLA *is restless. The* BARON *and* NIJINSKY *enter and* ROMOLA *ostentatiously raises her book to read. The* BARON *is laughing as* NIJINSKY *is imitating the* MAN WITH THE PIPE.*)*

BARON: Yes, yes that is him! I swear it is him down to the annoying way he holds his pipe. He is pretentious, isn't he? I don't know why the English are so determined to be thought eccentric. I mean, did he think it was attractive? All those bizarre stories about mysterious fires and prominent social figures beaten to death with polo mallets? I refuse to take him seriously.

NIJINSKY: He seemed to like you well enough.

BARON: Please! And when he said, "Dimitri, if you ever want to commit suicide, do it in my arms..." Oh, look, there's that lovely girl. Shall we say hello?

(The BARON doesn't wait for a response and heads over to ROMOLA who feigns distraction. NIJINSKY goes to the ship's rail. He is followed by the two prostitutes.)

BARON: What are you reading, my dear?

ROMOLA: Baron, you startled me.

(NIJINSKY smiles and approaches.)

ROMOLA: Anna Karenina.

(The BARON takes it and shows it to NIJINSKY.)

BARON: Look, she is reading a Russian novel, Anna Karenina, by Tolstoy.

NIJINSKY: *(Takes it rather brusquely and looks at it and gives it back. To BARON)* In French! *(To ROMOLA)* You love Tolstoy?

ROMOLA: Monsieur said something about Tolstoy?

(NIJINSKY and ROMOLA exchange smiles.)

BARON: He asked what you thought of the book.

ROMOLA: Actually, I'm very annoyed with Tolstoy— He made Anna Karenina into such a ninny.

NIJINSKY: *(To BARON)* She doesn't like Tolstoy. *(To ROMOLA)* Tolstoy, my hero!

BARON: I'm sure you misunderstood...

(NIJINSKY walks away and looks out to sea.)

BARON: *(To ROMOLA)* He speaks so little French.... Now where did he go? Let me introduce you.

ROMOLA: Never mind, Dimitri. He obviously is more interested in the ocean.

BARON: Oh, you know how he is...the artist.

ROMOLA: No, Baron, really don't bother.

BARON: Why? Are you afraid of him? He may be *Le Dieu de la Dance* on-stage, but off stage he's a charming young man.

ROMOLA: I'm not afraid of him.

BARON: Good. Then let me present him to you.

ROMOLA: I don't care to, Baron. Thank you.

BARON: Don't be silly. You admire him.

ROMOLA: Do I?

BARON: Please! He's captivating. We all admire him. He won't harm you. I promise.
We are great pals.

ROMOLA: No. I'm just sick of it. I've been presented to him over and over again and he never remembers me.

BARON: Vaslav Fomitch.

(NIJINSKY *approaches smiling.*)

BARON: So! Monsieur Nijinsky, *permettez-moi de vous presenter* Mademoiselle De Pulsky. Her mother is the greatest classical actress in Hungary.

(ROMOLA *extends her hand and* NIJINSKY *takes it.*)

BARON: *Mademoisellle* De Pulsky is a very talented dancer in our *corps de ballet.*

NIJINSKY: Yes.

ROMOLA: Yes...Yes...Oh! *Monsieur* Nijinsky, I must thank you.

NIJINSKY: Thank me?

ROMOLA: Oh, yes, for *Printemps,* for *Sacre.*

NIJINSKY: You are welcome.

ROMOLA: You've made dance the highest art. No matter what they say—never lose your nerve! Do you understand me?

(*The* BARON *begins to translate but* NIJINSKY *stops him.*)

ROMOLA: All great art begins as blasphemy!

NIJINSKY: Very interesting girl. She has many opinions.

BARON: Very astute and so well read...quite comfortable income.

ROMOLA: *(Looking straight at* NIJINSKY*)* So, gentlemen, do I meet with your approval this time?

(*They stare at each other.*)

BARON: Sorry. These language difficulties, you know...

NIJINSKY: I want to see her arch.

BARON: I can hardly ask her that!

NIJINSKY: Yes!

BARON: No.

NIJINSKY: *(To* ROMOLA*)* Please, *mademoiselle*—your foot.

BARON: He wants to examine your arch.

ROMOLA: I don't think so.

NIJINSKY: Please.

(NIJINSKY *kisses* ROMOLA's *hand.*)

ROMOLA: All right

(ROMOLA *extends her foot for* NIJINSKY *to take off her shoe. He does and examines her foot for flexibility. It is rather painful.*)

BARON: You know, I must tell you. We've decided to have a costume ball this evening to celebrate crossing the equator. I hope you'll come. Perhaps I shall be an *odalisque* and, Romola Carlovna, I have a brilliant idea for you. You are so slim. You almost look like a boy, *(He examines her.)* and if you hide your hair, I will loan you a pair of my green silk pajamas.

ROMOLA: And what will you wear, Monsieur Nijinsky?

(NIJINSKY *drops* ROMOLA's *foot. He stands gives a brief smile and bow and exits.*)

BARON: I hate artists! *(Laughs uneasily)* Yes, well, he's a bit rough around the edges. I shall have to mention that to him. Well then—when you write her—regards to your mother. Brrrrr—she's a real tiger, isn't she?

(ANNA *returns.*)

BARON: Good day, Anna. *(He exits.)*

ROMOLA: Anna, guess what? *Le Petit* came over and flirted with me and I looked into his eyes. They're slanted, just like my pet Siamese. His eyes aren't green as I thought on-stage. They're a soft, soft brown, like velvet.

(*Eyes appear in the sky like stars. As the lights darken, some are cat's eyes, others are human. Some stare, some blink. We see* NIJINSKY *asleep in his cabin.*)

(*End of Scene Three*)

Scene Four

(The giant eyes, blinking and non-blinking become even more pronounced. We can make out NIJINSKY's *figure lying on the bed and another figure in formal attire sitting at the foot of the bed. The figure reaches over and pours some water from a flask at* NIJINSKY's *bedside.* NIJINSKY *stirs. He is still dressed in his practice clothes and reaches blindly for the water.)*

DIAGHELIFF: Is this what you're looking for?

(NIJINSKY *is horrified and doesn't move.)*

DIAGHELIFF: One really shouldn't nap in the afternoon. It's such a heavy sleep and one becomes so disoriented, don't you think?

(DIAGHELIFF *hands the glass to* NIJINSKY *who drinks from it.)*

DIAGHELIFF: But my dear, you know you wanted to see me. Here. Drink. Drink.

NIJINSKY: You have a new boy anyway. Go away. *(He gulps down some water and lights some lights.)*

DIAGHELIFF: I'm still here. Of course, you are seeing things. Perhaps, you've lost control of your mind. Ah, *mon cher*, careful, you are beginning to remind me of your crazy brother, Stassik. Poor soul. *(He looks around the cabin.)* Those eyes are making me nervous. You're not becoming paranoid, are you?

(DIAGHELIFF *snaps his fingers and the eyes disappear.)*

NIJINSKY: I know what an eye is. An eye is a theater.

DIAGHELIFF: Shush, Vatza, shush.

NIJINSKY: I am sick at heart, Sergei. I am tired of intrigue and intrigue. I want to be an unnecessary man. I want to be a monk and build a simple house. I want to go to Siberia and preach to the peasants and work the land. I want to be a tree and its roots. I want to live simply, in isolation.

DIAGHELIFF: You must stop reading that old lunatic, Tolstoy. All this "philosophy".
You are getting so boring, Vatza. I want you to take some time off, but for God's sake, use it creatively. Remember we must do something astonishing for Paris next year. Tolstoy! You would go back to the Stone Age at a time when we can't afford to be less modern. No! Futurism, cubism—the soul splintered from the universe—these are the last words. I will not let the position of artistic leadership slip away from me.

NIJINSKY: It's too late. You've already become the ultimate lackey a servile follower, you, the visionary, are now terrified of causing the least scandal.

DIAGHELIFF: You only say this because I thought your ballet *Jeux* was a complete failure. Even your *Sacre du Printemps* is not a real ballet... And *L'Apres Midi*—an eleven-minute ballet that needs a hundred hours of rehearsal. My God. All our friends of the Ballets Russes agree with me. It would be a mistake to encourage you further as a choreographer.

NIJINSKY: *Jeux* was not entirely successful. But, *Sacre* was important.

DIAGHELIFF: The public, the paying public booed it.

NIJINSKY: It's new. It was not understood.

DIAGHELIFF: Vatza, Vatza. A painting or a piece of music might be misunderstood at first or unappreciated for a long time, maybe a hundred years, but a ballet? A ballet must be received by the public today or else it is doomed to obscurity. Come, come I have given you three ballets to choreograph and they are simply not the kind of Ballets that can sustain the success of the Ballets Russes. You must understand that I have a great obligation.

NIJINSKY: But not to me.

DIAGHELIFF: Of course to you, darling. In fact I want you to look at some new ballets Fokine is choreographing and give me your opinion.

NIJINSKY: Fokine?

DIAGHELIFF: Yes. That is, if you have time. I must remember to tell that idiot, De Gunsbourg, to keep the little Hungarian flirt away from you. That imbecile. Does he really think he can separate the two of us with a socialite? He's plotting to have his own company again, but I am hardly worried. That man couldn't run a flea circus.

NIJINSKY: I don't think as little of women as you do, Sergei.

DIAGHELIFF: My poor little saint. How you suffer.

NIJINSKY: There is a difference between what I do for others and what I do for myself.

(*Two* DANCERS *dressed as prostitutes dance out laughing raucously and approach first* NIJINSKY *and then turn to fawn over* DIAGHELIFF, *who treats them with bored indifference.*)

DIAGHELIFF: Really?

NIJINSKY: Those long solitary walks in Paris? I was looking for whores. I wanted beautiful, healthy girls. I fucked whores every day. Once I made love to a woman who had her period. I was covered with it. Then I went to you because I knew it would disgust you. I lied to you. I became you, a fake, a fraud. You dye your hair black so no one will know you are old, but I know you're old. I see that disgusting black cream you leave on the pillowcases and the lock of hair you dye white just to be noticed—it has turned yellow. Yellow. You have two false front teeth and when you take them out, you look like a wicked old woman. And that monocle you wear is only for effect. Your eyes are perfect. Deceit is your art. Deceit and sex.

DIAGHELIFF: You didn't seem to mind the sex, as I recall. Actually, as I was telling Prince Lvov when he passed you on to me, I was quite gratified by all the nice tricks he taught you. He was a very athletic young man, wasn't he?

NIJINSKY: He understood love. He wrote love poems. He was beautiful. He thought you would be useful to me.

DIAGHELIFF: Yes. His was a great love. He passed you around like a used penny. And I—who corrupted you, who used you—as you claim—made you a god. *Le dieu de la danse.* Vatza, you are a great artist, a gentle soul. Who else can appreciate you as I do?

NIJINSKY: You appreciate me like a painting in a museum. Museums are graveyards!
They are tidy. They are dead. Beauty for me isn't tidy. It's not pretty. Beauty is feeling in a face. Beauty is a hunchback. I like ugly people. I am an ugly man with feeling. I dance hunchbacks and straight-backs. I am the artist who loves all shapes and all kinds of beauty.

DIAGHELIFF: Then you must love me, too.

NIJINSKY: I have found a girl. She has chestnut hair, her nose is long and straight. It has character. Her eyes are alive. I want to fuck her.

DIAGHELIFF: What are you doing, Vatza? I am worried to death about you.

NIJINSKY: Of course. You, who thought I was boring and stupid. Who was ashamed I would speak and humiliate you in front of your brilliant friends. I hated you. But I loved the Ballets Russes. I gave my whole heart to the Ballets Russes. I worked like an ox. I lived like a martyr. I killed myself for the dance, but I am tired. Tired. So tired of you showing that Nijinsky is your pupil in everything. I was tired of looking for love when there was nothing. You love fame, you love boys, you love a beautiful body, and you love *objets d'art.* You are wicked. You are crazy. I carry you with me like a stone, like a cross I can't put down. Leave me alone so I can breathe. I am going to the New World. I will have a new life and will do what God asks me.

(DIAGHELIFF *exits.* VASSILY *enters.*)

VASSILY: Vatza,Vatza. *(He fills a glass with water.)* Here drink. There is nothing to be afraid of. Nothing.

NIJINSKY: *(Sobbing)* You are not wicked. I will weep for you if you are ever hurt. I do not like you, but you are a human being and I love all human beings. I have no right to judge. The judge is God and he will whisper in my ear what to do, what to do...

VASSILY: Shall I make more light in the room?

NIJINSKY: What? No.

VASSILY: Here, let me wipe your face. You're sweating. You had a dream? You had a nightmare? ...There...there...all will be well, you'll see. Do you want to go to the costume ball? Yes? Shall I lay out your choices. You should never sleep in the afternoon. It is a heavy, unhealthy sleep. I will open a porthole. Here...drink Vatza. Water will cleanse you.

(End of Scene Four)

Scene Five

(The party. We hear music. A crowd gathers. A tango is begun. Suddenly, we see a figure spotlighted center stage. The figure is dressed in classic tango clothes. However, only the right half is dressed as a man, the left half is dressed as a woman; we believe it is only a man dancing. There is a dramatic turn and then the female side is turned toward the audience. The man/woman does a solo tango in which he first seduce some of the dancers as a man and then the other as a woman. Then the three pair off with the other passengers. They all tango. This dance should last about two minutes.)

(As the tango is ending, NIJINSKY enters. He is not in costume but in evening clothes looking very elegant. The lights come up and we see a circle of grotesquely costumed party goers. DIAGHELIFF with the large papier-maché head is there also. Someone is dressed as a bird of paradise and another as a gargoyle with a goat head. NIJINSKY is very interested in the steps of the tango.)

(The tango ends and a bolero begins. Couples pair off. The DIAGHELIFF head approaches NIJINSKY. The head is removed and we see the BARON underneath.)

BARON: Good evening. Good evening. How handsome you look, but you're not in costume. Or are you? Let me guess, you're disguised as a gentleman. Just joking. Just joking. As you can see, I've come as a monster our dear Sergei. Speaking of which, I hope you are accepting my proposal. You could work independently. We could build a new theater. Didn't you say you wanted a round theater like the Greeks?

NIJINSKY: Like an eye.

BARON: Yes. Yes. An eye. An eye. Exactly, the cyclopean eye, all seeing. Brilliant. Well, no business. When I hear music...ah...I simply must dance. Do I look like an idiot? Don't tell me if I do. I'm having too much fun!

(The BARON disappears into the crowd and grabs a partner. ROMOLA enters alone. She is wearing an elegant evening dress and her hair is carefully done. She and NIJINSKY nod to each other, but stand silently a little ways apart watching the crowd. Finally, NIJINSKY moves closer.)

NIJINSKY: Good evening, *mademoiselle*.

ROMOLA: Good evening, Monsieur Nijinsky.

(There is much gesturing and pantomime between them to make themselves understood.)

NIJINSKY: Beautiful dress.

ROMOLA: Thank you.

NIJINSKY: No costume...

ROMOLA: I want to feel pretty, not disguised.

NIJINSKY: For me—Too much costume—always clown, slave, flower—tragic. Tonight only myself.

ROMOLA: Me too.

(ROMOLA *and* NIJINSKY *smile at each other. They are silent and watch the dance then. They both speak at once.)*

ROMOLA: Do you enjoy...

NIJINSKY: I must tell you.

ROMOLA: Go on. You must tell me... What?

NIJINSKY: No you.

ROMOLA: All right. Do you enjoy this Argentine music?

NIJINSKY: Very much. I learn tango. Very dramatic. You teach?

ROMOLA: I don't know it. I've never been to Buenos Aires before.

(The half-man, half-woman approaches NIJINSKY.*)*

MAN/WOMAN: Senor Nijinsky, I am so honored. I want to prostrate myself before the altar of your magnificence. I want to tell you how noble, how utterly handsome and graceful you are, yet inexorably masculine. Your greatness humbles us all.

NIJINSKY: *(To* ROMOLA*)* I'm sorry...

ROMOLA: She said she was delighted to meet you.

NIJINSKY: *(He extends his hand, which the* MAN/WOMAN *grabs and kisses.)* You dance very good.

MAN/WOMAN: I hear you love all dances. The tango is queen among dances and, if you like, I will teach you. Yes?

(They look at ROMOLA.*)*

ROMOLA: She'd like to teach you to tango. You see, what you wish for comes true.

NIJINSKY: Now?

ROMOLA: Yes.

*(*ROMOLA *and* NIJINSKY *stare at each other and reach a silent agreement.)*

NIJINSKY: I love to learn, but later. Tell her please.

ROMOLA: Of course, he'd love to dance, but later.

MAN/WOMAN: Later then. *(She turns the masculine side to him and then the feminine side.)* You can dance with whomever pleases you most. *(She exits.)*

ROMOLA: She said later is fine.

NIJINSKY: You speak Spanish?

ROMOLA: A little.

NIJINSKY: My French—terrible, like savage. You speak Russian?

ROMOLA: Not a word. I don't suppose you speak Hungarian?

NIJINSKY: I am sorry.

ROMOLA: I'm Hungarian. From Budapest.

NIJINSKY: Am Polish and Russian.

ROMOLA: My father's family is from Poland.

NIJINSKY: You speak Polish? I speak Polish.

ROMOLA: No. My father's family left Poland a hundred years ago.

NIJINSKY: Ah.

ROMOLA: Yes.

(They fall silent again. NIJINSKY *offers* ROMOLA *his arm.)*

NIJINSKY: Shall we? Away from lights, see sky better.

*(*ROMOLA *is enchanted. She takes* NIJINSKY's *arm. They walk a few steps, but it is the dancers who sweep offstage, leaving them alone. The stars brighten and the music grows faint.)*

ROMOLA: Have we crossed... *(Gestures)* Crossed the equator?

NIJINSKY: Yes.

ROMOLA: Then, this is a new sky I've never seen before.

NIJINSKY: The New World.

ROMOLA: They say there are new constellations. New stars that can't be seen from the Northern Hemisphere.

NIJINSKY: You know stars?

ROMOLA: No. Do you know constellations?

NIJINSKY: No.

(ROMOLA *and* NIJINSKY *are quiet, smiling for a moment. She turns away and crosses herself.*)

ROMOLA: Thank you Divine Mother.

NIJINSKY: What this?

ROMOLA: Nothing.

NIJINSKY: Tell me, you love dance?

ROMOLA: Dance? Oh dance. I'm only in the chorus.

NIJINSKY: But Ballet Russes chorus! Good. You love dance?

ROMOLA: I adore dance, but...

NIJINSKY: If comes from heart—is good. Others more virtuosi. Yes. But heart give grace.

ROMOLA: If it were only heart you needed! But you work hard at it. Endlessly. I hoped...I thought that grace might be acquired.

NIJINSKY: Ac-quired?

ROMOLA: Learned.

NIJINSKY: Ah yes. Hard work. Good. But grace learned is only little. Grace born. Grace born has no end...

ROMOLA: I should so want grace, limitless grace.

NIJINSKY: So serious. But now we laugh. I show you Dimitri. So vain in his looks—because has none. Now Dimitri in love... Here come man with pipe... (*He mimics* BARON.) I do perfect Dimitri. No?

ROMOLA: Yes. A splendid Dimitri!

(NIJINSKY *walks away suddenly.*)

NIJINSKY: I'm sick of lies.

ROMOLA: What lies?

NIJINSKY: You here with me because I am famous.

ROMOLA: No!

NIJINSKY: Yes. World imitates. Foolish women put eyes like this *(Indicates slanted eyes.)* With black pencil so look like me...ahhh Nijinsky. Ballets Russes— Ooooh-la-la. I am rich now. Famous. If not—you never here!

ROMOLA: How rude!

(ROMOLA turns to leave. NIJINSKY steps in front of her.)

NIJINSKY: Tell me truth.

ROMOLA: The truth?

NIJINSKY: Yes.

ROMOLA: Fine then. The truth. When I first saw you—you were already rich and famous—so I can't say what I'd have done if you'd been different!

NIJINSKY: Ah!

ROMOLA: Did you understand?

NIJINSKY: Yes. Say again.

ROMOLA: Why?

NIJINSKY: Please.

ROMOLA: I said that when I first say you—you were already rich and famous—so I have no idea what I'd have done if you'd been different.

NIJINSKY: Again!

ROMOLA: Again?

NIJINSKY: Yes. Exact words.

ROMOLA: Why?

NIJINSKY: Like music to me. I love truth. I love this truth.

ROMOLA: What about you? You probably think I am very rich?

NIJINSKY: Yes.

ROMOLA: I'm not very rich. Only a little.

(NIJINSKY laughs.)

NIJINSKY: Yes. Yes. *(He is smiling.)*

ROMOLA: What?

NIJINSKY: Now we like Tolstoy and wife Sofia.

ROMOLA: So you've forgiven me Tolstoy?

NIJINSKY: Tolstoy love truth. With truth—open heart. Simple life. Tolstoy and Sofia—write everything...write, write...every morning.

ROMOLA: They kept diaries.

NIJINSKY: Yes. Every night read out loud—everything, good, bad. All. I love this. Peace. And you?

ROMOLA: I don't think I can be so mercilessly candid.

NIJINSKY: Yes. Is possible. Maybe...I begin. No secrets. I am Catholic because born Polish. But really am Russian. Russian soul—eat bread, cabbage soup. I love Russia. I miss Russia too much.

ROMOLA: I'm Catholic too.

NIJINSKY: Yes! Yes! ...But...

ROMOLA: But what? Tell me everything.

NIJINSKY: My mother...her mother...

ROMOLA: *(Trying to follow his train of thought)* Your grandmother.

NIJINSKY: Yes. My grandmother die, starve herself. Die screaming.

ROMOLA: How terrible.

NIJINSKY: You must know!

ROMOLA: What?

NIJINSKY: Stassik, my brother...is crazy...ugly. Perhaps I too am... *(He stops, corrects himself. Smiles. He imitates Stassik)* ...am good mimic, but great dancer. In dance, I make Stassik beautiful. We talk dance. You are dancer. I must see you dance. If dance, must dance beautifully. I give lessons so you dance more beautifully.

ROMOLA: No. No. I would never even think to ask you.

NIJINSKY: I am not critic. I am teacher. I hate critics. Critics think public is stupid.
Critics think to explain art to stupid public. I hate critic. Critic is death.
(He loses himself in thought.)

ROMOLA: *Monsieur* Nijinsky?

NIJINSKY: Yes.

ROMOLA: Are you all right?

NIJINSKY: I want to say to you, before.

ROMOLA: Yes? What were you going to say?

NIJINSKY: You have beautiful eyes, but is nose I like.

ROMOLA: My nose?

NIJINSKY: *(He kisses her nose.)* Has character. Now know why. Is good straight Polish nose.

(A couple from the dance strolls by. Then the rest of the dancers, a bit inebriated, sweep in. The BARON, *disengages himself and approaches* ROMOLA *and* NIJINSKY.*)*

BARON: Where have you been? You don't know what a stir you've caused. Everyone is talking. So interested. So worried. You, Romuschka are a gold digger and you, Vaslav are a fickle flirt...or is it the other way around?

ROMOLA: I'm afraid that I have a headache that's quite painful. I must find Anna.

BARON: What? I have said something terrible. Don't go. Ignore me. Ah, but, Vatza, can you imagine Sergei? He would be livid. He would be drunk with so many of his English scotches by now, but so polite. He'd kill you with politeness. Thank God, none of us have to worry. He's not here. He's terrified of boats and the ocean. My, ever since a gypsy told him he would die at sea...

NIJINSKY: Excuse, *Mademoiselle*, Baron.

(He goes to the MAN/WOMAN *and asks her to dance. She begins to teach him the tango. The prostitutes also set themselves to learn.)*

BARON: My dear, you must tell me about your evening. Are you in love?

ROMOLA: I must go to bed, Dimitri.

BARON: You're magic together!

ROMOLA: Forgive me.

BARON: But I haven't told you about the other gossip. Poor Maicherska. Did you see?
She insisted on displaying her lovely shoulders, even with a tremendous love bite on one of them. She tried to say that a washstand had fallen on her, but no one believed her.

ROMOLA: You must tell me everything. Tomorrow!

BARON: *(As he exits with* ROMOLA*)* I won't hear of it. I shall walk you to your cabin.
But, did you hear? One of the busboys cut off the last digit of his ring finger to impress his girlfriend? Such cries...

(The BARON *exits with* ROMOLA.*)*

(End of Scene Five)

Scene Six

(ROMOLA *is in her cabin, happy and excited with the evening. She changes into her dressing gown and goes to hang up her dress. She opens a closet, or parts some clothes and there is* EMILIA, *dressed as Ophelia.*)

EMILIA: Well? Who am I?

ROMOLA: Mother!

EMILIA: No, no, no. You know the game. Who am I?

ROMOLA: I'm no longer a child.

EMILIA: That's debatable. But let's not quibble. This is such a good game. Indulge me or I won't go away. Who am I?

ROMOLA: You're Ophelia from The Royal Theater's 1912 production of Hamlet. A very old Ophelia.

EMILIA: If you look as good at my age, you will kneel down and kiss the earth with gratitude. Now what did I do?

ROMOLA: You murdered my father.

EMILIA: Your father killed himself. But I am talking about the play. In the play, what did Ophelia do?

ROMOLA: She died for love. It wasn't reciprocated.

EMILIA: Just like you. I rest my case.

ROMOLA: Like my father.

EMILIA: What would you know? You were a child. Your father was unstable and unpredictable. On a good day, I would say he was a tragic figure, sort of a Don Quixote with a dim sense of reality. On a bad day, I would call him a fool. And when he was drunk...I hated it when Karoly was drunk and wanted to make love...now why are we getting into this?

ROMOLA: We always do.

EMILIA: That's not why I'm here.

ROMOLA: Why are you here?

EMILIA: I won't have you chasing after a man you can never catch. You may despise me, but I am your mother and I warn you, as your mother and as a woman of the world, that Nijinsky's friendship with Diagheliff is more than a friendship. He can't possibly be interested in you!

ROMOLA: Mother—Diagheliff is his past. Perhaps *Le Petit* needs something different now... Why shouldn't I be the one to provide Nijinsky with a future? After all, Diagheliff cannot bear his children!

EMILIA: Oh superb, now you aspire to be a cow's udder.

ROMOLA: Of course that would be how you see mothering...mother! Public acclaim is not my only measure of success.

EMILIA: I don't see you chasing after a bricklayer.

ROMOLA: I aspire to be a person of flesh and blood and heart. I will be passionate and loyal. I will never refuse to go to my husband when he needs me most.

EMILIA: As I did?

ROMOLA: Oh, I understand, Mama. Father was in Australia and, of course, you couldn't go there, could you? After all, you can only act in Hungarian, and Mother—no one understand Hungarian!

EMILIA: All right, then hate me—but don't be a fool.

ROMOLA: Like my father!

EMILIA: Romola!

ROMOLA: Divine Jesus of Prague...please...please...please save me from this horrid woman.

EMILIA: *(Imitates* ROMOLA *scathingly)* Please... Please... Divine Child...

ROMOLA: Go away!

(ROMOLA *exits.* ANNA *enters.*)

ANNA: Go away? Go away? And here I thought you wanted to know if your precious Vaslav was on deck. Well he is, and for your information, you only have ten more days to steal his heart. And you needn't be rude to me because you're in a bad mood!

(End of Scene Six)

Scene Seven

(Morning on deck. People coming and going from breakfast. The captain and one of the dancers enter. She is dressed very bohemian for that time. Lots of jewelry and a funky hat)

BOHEMIAN WOMAN: My concepts of society are more developed now. I look at Karl Marx as a very intelligent charismatic revolutionary.

CAPTAIN: Wasn't Karl Marx a Jew?

BOHEMIAN WOMAN: I'm not recanting.

(The BARON arrives.)

CAPTAIN: Good morning, Baron.

BARON: Morning, morning.

CAPTAIN: When you sit down, ask for the fresh oranges. Wonderful. Those monkeys in Sicily picked them.

BARON: Gibraltar has the monkeys. Sicily has the oranges.

CAPTAIN: My mistake. I thought those little dark creatures picking oranges in Sicily were monkeys. *(He laughs alone.)*

(CAPTAIN and the dancer exit.)

(ANNA arrives and then RUPERT close behind her. He offers her a single flower. The BARON sees this and stands there glaring at him.)

ANNA: Rupert. How dear of you. I hope you slept well.

RUPERT: Why is that man staring at me?

ANNA: Perhaps he thinks he knows you.

(ANNA gives a little wave to the BARON, who looks away.)

ANNA: That's Baron de Gunsbourg. He's quite charming, I assure you.

RUPERT: He seems odd, but no matter. How would you like to stroll with me and watch the sun dancing fire off the waves?

ANNA: I'd love to, but I haven't had breakfast yet.

RUPERT: Yes, I see.

ANNA: I'm not rejecting you.

RUPERT: Good. Then, perhaps later this morning.

ANNA: That would be lovely.

RUPERT: Your English is astonishingly good.

ANNA: Why thank you.

RUPERT: Yes, well... Shall I accompany you to breakfast?

ANNA: Why yes.

RUPERT: May I watch you eat?

ANNA: What?

RUPERT: I just thought... The truth is, I find your mouth delectable and want to watch you...well, move it.

ANNA: You're making me quite self-conscious.

RUPERT: Sorry.

ANNA: Yes.

RUPERT: Should I go then?

ANNA: You can stay, but don't stare at my mouth.

RUPERT: Oh, no. I wouldn't think of it.

(ANNA *is a bit distracted.*)

RUPERT: There is a favor I'd like to ask.

ANNA: Yes.

RUPERT: The question's been bothering me. Kept me up nights. What a puzzle. And you, being a woman, well, I'm sure you would know this sort of thing.

ANNA: I'd love to help.

RUPERT: Such fine elocution from such a lovely mouth. Sorry. I got carried away. Sorry.

ANNA: Yes.

RUPERT: The question I have is this—well, it's something my aunty told me. She said women stuff all kinds of sweet things inside themselves so animals will lick them down there. Is that true?

ANNA: What!?

(ANNA *slaps* RUPERT's *face and starts to leave.*)

RUPERT: I'll take that as a no.

(ANNA *hurries off to* ROMOLA's *cabin. To* ROMOLA *angrily—*)

ANNA: Loving someone you don't know is a knife in the heart. But I suppose—if a man is twisted or damaged—it is better to know that now.

(ROMOLA *comforts her.*)

(*End of Scene Seven*)

Scene Eight

(ROMOLA *and* ANNA *are in* ROMOLA's *cabin getting ready to go to breakfast.* VASSILY *approaches with a large bouquet of white roses. Two maids rush by, one is carrying clean towels.*)

VASSILY: *(Muttering.)* It will be me! Me! I will be the one who answers the door and lies to her annoying face that you're not in! What do you care if you tire of her or not? Everyone wants to see you, meet you, touch you. *(Spits)* What am I, a doorman, a pimp? Wait! You'll see her dance, your heart will drop to your boots and I, Vassily, am here to pick it up and slam the door in her face. Achhh...

(VASSILY *knocks loudly on* ROMOLA's *door.* ANNA *answers.*)

ANNA: Yes?

VASSILY: *(He thrusts the flowers into her arms.)* Here!

(VASSILY *walks away a few paces.* ANNA *closes the door, a bit puzzled. She looks for a note.*)

ROMOLA: Who is it?

ANNA: Vassily.

ROMOLA: Oh, let me see. What beautiful roses Anna. You see? I've caught Nijinsky's eye. Isn't it wonderful? Next I'll catch his heart.

(VASSILY *knocks again at the door.* ROMOLA *jumps up.* ANNA *opens it. He hands her an envelope. As* ANNA *goes to shut the door, he holds it open.*)

VASSILY: She is very sly, but I know what she is up to. I see everything. How she talks louder when he enters a room so he'll notice her. How she waits to come out her door until he's in the hallway. She can never understand him. Never. He was born to dance. She is nothing. She will never know his true heart. My God, she will ruin him. Sergei Diagheliff will have a heart attack. It is the end of the Ballets Russes. *Finis! (He is almost in tears. He exits.)*

ANNA: *(Yells after him.)* Moujik! *(She slams the door.)*

ROMOLA: What did he say?

ANNA: Don't ask me. I don't understand a word of that barbaric language. All I understood was *"finis"* and he gave me this. It's for you, of course.

ROMOLA: *"Finis? Finis?"* What does he mean finished?

ANNA: Go ahead. Read it to me.

ROMOLA: Just a minute. *(She smells it.)* Mmm. It has his cologne, Guerlain, I believe.

ANNA: I prefer the smell of pipe tobacco and a good energetic walk around the deck. *(Referring to the note)* If the French is good, you can be sure the Baron wrote it.

ROMOLA: Oh.

ANNA: What does it say?

ROMOLA: He says "forgive me". But I have nothing to forgive him for. What could he mean? He's sorry he kissed me. He won't be seeing me again. "*Finis.*" "*Finis.*" What else could it mean?

ANNA: Ask him.

ROMOLA: I can't face him.

ANNA: I can't stand it. Let's go to breakfast. Please. I'm starving and Nijinsky has already left. I heard his door close.

ROMOLA: I'll die if he ignores me when I pass his table. I'll know he meant good-bye.
And after they all saw us alone together. The humiliation. Everyone will see it. No, I can't possibly go.

ANNA: Young love is so enervating. You really must come out and eat something.

ROMOLA: You go. At least I can practice. I must practice. I must dance.

(ANNA *exits as* ROMOLA *begins to practice. She starts with some hesitant steps from* Les Sylphides. *The two women dancers come out in classic white tutus and proceed to dance* Sylphides *beautifully.* ROMOLA *tries to keep up with them. She can't. She watches sadly and then exits. This dance should be almost a minute and a half.)*

END OF ACT ONE

ACT TWO

Scene One

(It is late night. ROMOLA *is pacing the deck. A couple passes sees her and starts whispering. She turns away and cries silently. The* CAPTAIN *with a bottle of champagne rushes through, stops for a minute, unsure if he should go to* ROMOLA *or not. Decides better of it and exits.* ROMOLA *sits on a deck chair in the dark and lights a cigarette.* NIJINSKY *enters.)*

NIJINSKY: *Mademoiselle!*

ROMOLA: *(Startled, she is torn between wanting to run away and putting out her cigarette. She does neither.)* Go away.

NIJINSKY: Romola.

ROMOLA: What?!

NIJINSKY: Smoke, no good for dance. *(Mimes coughing)*

ROMOLA: Leave if it bothers you. *(She turns so he can't see her face. She blows a plume of smoke.)*

NIJINSKY: Eyes red.

ROMOLA: Please, *Monsieur* Nijinsky.

NIJINSKY: You like me little, so can't say, Vaslav?

ROMOLA: We hardly know each other.

NIJINSKY: True. We walk and know better.

ROMOLA: No, thank you. *(She puts out her cigarette.)*

NIJINSKY: You cry?

ROMOLA: No.

NIJINSKY: I see. But, I think you cry. I think. I think... *(He kisses her lightly.)* You cry for me?

ROMOLA: Yes. So?

NIJINSKY: We walk.

ROMOLA: Please spare me. Well, leave! Or do you think I'm so desperate that common decency won't work with me? You're probably right, I'm like one of those silly girls who steal your underwear after a performance. And yes, I've done that too. I've rummaged around in your hotel at Monte Carlo—like an opium addict after cash... I snatched a little pillow they said your mother made which you slept on every night. So there! I stole it! I sleep with it. So—laugh at me!

NIJINSKY: *(Laughing)* I'm sorry. You speak too fast. You love a pillow?

ROMOLA: You're impossible. You understood every word I said.

NIJINSKY: No. Please, please. Not words. But, you I understand. I feel you. You feel me, too, no? So.

(NIJINSKY *takes* ROMOLA's *hand and puts it through his arm. They walk. he points to the sky.*)

NIJINSKY: That? So bright. The Southern Cross. See, I have learned. New World.

(They watch the sky in silence for a moment. We hear the water against the hull of the moving ship.)

NIJINSKY: Modern people say no God. Everything "little pieces in motion". I believe in God. Some people God wants... *(Gestures)* ...together. In the Stars. *(He holds their hands out together. He points to her ring finger, and then to his.)* Romola?

ROMOLA: Yes.

NIJINSKY: Do you want? *Voulez-vous? Vous et moi?*

ROMOLA: You and I?

NIJINSKY: Yes.

ROMOLA: Married?

NIJINSKY: *Oui.*

(Extended pause between them. A group of four approach. Three women draping themselves over the arm of a tall man in a top hat. The women are laughing.)

NIJINSKY: You first woman I love.

ROMOLA: The very first?

NIJINSKY: Yes.

ROMOLA: I don't believe you.

NIJINSKY: Truth.

ROMOLA: But you're in such carefree company with so many beautiful women!

NIJINSKY: But only you. Only. *(He kisses her hand.) Voulez-vous? Vous et moi? ...Oui?*

ROMOLA: Yes. Oh yes. I'll marry you!

(NIJINSKY kisses ROMOLA's hand again, then kisses her.)

ROMOLA: But when?

NIJINSKY: Now. Buenos Aires. Sacred. In church.

ROMOLA: Yes. In church. A dress! I have no papers! *(She embraces him.)* I knew you had a kind heart. I saw you dance so many, many times. I knew your genius, your nature, everything! Anyone who dances as you do must have a loving heart!

NIJINSKY: I am sorry...

ROMOLA: But, *Monsieur*...what do you want from me?

NIJINSKY: From you...?

ROMOLA: *Monsieur.*

NIJINSKY: Yes?

ROMOLA: Why did you write "forgive me" on the note with your flowers?

NIJINSKY: *(Laughs)* Dark mood. Russian mood. But at heart—am joyous Pole. So! Now—only beautiful notes. I go write—dancing like Pavlova. *(He imitates Pavolva and glides offstage.)*

(End of Scene One)

Scene Two

(ROMOLA is trying on dresses. ANNA is helping her. ANNA exits. EMILIA enters, dressed exotically and tragically as Medea.)

EMILIA: Ouff—don't tell me you're wearing blue. It's very unlucky.

ROMOLA: For the love of God!

EMILIA: You know who I am today, or do I need to show you my bloody knife?

ROMOLA: Why would you come to my marriage as Medea, mother?

EMILIA: Marriage can be vicious.

ROMOLA: You're jealous because I've proven you wrong. He can love me. He does love me.

EMILIA: I wouldn't wear blue if I were you.

(EMILIA *drifts offstage crossing paths with two ballerinas who rush in.*)

BALLERINA I: Katrina is having hysterics because Nijinsky is marrying you. And, with all the men on board, she has to faint in my husband's arms.

BALLERINA II: Congratulations! I am so happy. So happy for you. I always knew Nijinsky wasn't like that. Let me see your ring.

(*She does.*)

BALLERINA II: Very pretty.

BALLERINA I: For my part, I would rather be a mistress. The Aga Kahn sent Marushka seven leopard skins and a ruby belt because she had the sniffles. Of course, Marushka is a *prima ballerina*.

BALLERINA II: Ouff! Don't tell me you're wearing blue. That's very unlucky.

(*They exit whispering together and* ANNA *returns with some pins to pin up the dress.*)

ROMOLA: I can't stand that dress.

ANNA: Why not? We're almost finished.

ROMOLA: I hate it. I won't wear it. Blue is bad luck.

ANNA: So, now you're superstitious?

ROMOLA: Now is not the time to tempt the gods. I want the white dress. With ropes of pearls.

ANNA: Well, you can't wear pearls.

ROMOLA: Why not?

ANNA: Some say they're unlucky too.

ROMOLA: Then I won't get married at all. Forget it!

ANNA: You don't mean that.

ROMOLA: Why not? I'm frightened. What's going to happen? Who knows what marriage is! I know—I'll write a note. Yes—find me some note paper. I'll write him. Ah, yes, I'll begin... "Forgive me..."

ANNA: Don't be ridiculous. It's only nerves.

ROMOLA: But it's not! What's the use? It's a farce.

ANNA: Roma—he loves you.

ROMOLA: But he hasn't seen me dance.

(ANNA *exits and returns with a cream-colored dress. At first,* ROMOLA *refuses to put it on, but then grudgingly lets* ANNA *dress her.*)

(NIJINSKY *in his wedding tuxedo takes him place on one corner of the stage. The priest appears in the center.* EMILIA *enters still dressed as Medea.*)

EMILIA: September 10, 1913. The first marriage—*le mariage du coeur.* Ladies and gentlemen, *(Indicating the wedding)* the Tower of Babel. The priest is speaking Latin; Romola, Hungarian; *Le Petit* Nijinsky, Polish. I have a headache and I'm not even invited.

(As EMILIA *exits, a vast shower of flower petals fall. The dancers enter carrying small lights which they place on the floor.* ROMOLA *has put on an extraordinarily long veil which trails behind her. She takes her place in another corner of the stage. As she and* NIJINSKY *speak, they walk towards each other. They are extremely happy.)*

ROMOLA: I, Romola, will stay with you, Vaslav, in happiness and misfortune, in health and sickness till death do us part

NIJINSKY: I, Vaslav, will stay with you, Romola, in happiness and misfortune, in health and sickness till death do us part.

(They exchange rings.)

PRIEST: In the name of The Father, The Son, and The Holy Spirit, I now pronounce you man and wife. Let no man put asunder whom God has joined today.

(They kiss. NIJINSKY *carries* ROMOLA *to the hotel room. There is a splendidly made up bed and an ornate chair with a robe lying over it and some books on the floor. The dancers scamper ahead and explore* NIJINSKY's *hotel room, bounce on the bed and look in every corner. One picks up a book that is lying around. The other one slaps her and takes it away and puts it back. They exit annoyed with each other.)*

(End of Scene Two)

Scene Three

(Hotel suite in Buenos Aires. ROMOLA *and* NIJINSKY *enter.)*

NIJINSKY: *(With grand gesture)* Honeyroom.

ROMOLA: *(Laughing)* Honey-moon.

(They laugh together. ROMOLA *looks over everything, touches a wall, a chair, etc.* NIJINSKY *watches. She comes to a robe draped over the bed and some books nearby.)*

NIJINSKY: I have champagne.

*(*NIJINSKY *exits to get it.* ROMOLA *touches his things—the valise, smells his robe, picks up one of the books to look at it. He enters with an open bottle and glasses. She takes them from him and fills the glasses.)*

ROMOLA: Let me pour.

NIJINSKY: *(He kisses her neck.) Maia jena.*

ROMOLA: What does that mean?

NIJINSKY: My wife.

(ROMOLA *and* NIJINSKY *smile at each other. He dips a finger in the Champagne and traces a cross on her forehead.)*

NIJINSKY: My mother always bless. "Christ be with you."

ROMOLA: And also with you.

NIJINSKY: Ah yes...and "Together forever through fire and water"!

ROMOLA: Is that holy too.

NIJINSKY: No. Polish.

ROMOLA: *(She dips her finger in the Champagne and makes the sing of the cross over his heart.)* "May this blessing preserve you from all evil". There! You're safe! My family says that—in Hungarian mind you!

(ROMOLA *and* NIJINSKY *sip their champagne.)*

ROMOLA: Now what shall we do?

NIJINSKY: We marry fast. Now—slow. slow. Roma, Romuscka, I have plan.

ROMOLA: Tell me.

NIJINSKY: Four years I dance, I live only for art. Then five years go to Russia, make a school, make children, make real family. I think is very good. And you?

ROMOLA: It's a wonderful plan. I'm so happy. We'll travel and entertain. We'll read Russian novels and tour museums and, of course, I will dress extravagantly well. And so will you— *(She brings over the robe.)* Put on the present I bought you. I want to see how you look!

NIJINSKY: Yes.

(As NIJINSKY *tries on the robe* ROMOLA *looks through the books.)*

ROMOLA: Does it fit? Put it on. No. You have to take your jacket off first. There. *(She puts down the book and helps him.)* Now your bowtie... *(She helps him.)* ...and your cummerbund...no, I'll let you do that.

(NIJINSKY *takes off his cummerbund and puts on the robe.)*

ROMOLA: You look like an emperor...I know...the emperor of Mongolia!

(ROMOLA *pulls the skin near her eyes to make them slant. They both laugh. She holds up the book.)*

ROMOLA: Is this yours?

NIJINSKY: Yes.

(NIJINSKY *goes to take it from* ROMOLA.)

ROMOLA: I want to see what you're reading.

NIJINSKY: Better no.

ROMOLA: I want to know all about you! I'm your wife now. And it's only a book. Oh! A picture book. It's Chinese. How exotic.

(*One of the dancers steals in and reads over her shoulder. The other dancer comes in shyly, curious.*)

NIJINSKY: It is very old.

ROMOLA: Look how beautiful it's made. All the figures are hand painted. The writing's so black, but it's Chinese. I can't read it.

(*The two dancers assume an obviously sexual pose and then contort into another. They laugh and run off as* ROMOLA *says.*)

ROMOLA: They're having sex!

NIJINSKY: I wanted for... You are offended.

ROMOLA: No. It's funny. It's fascinating...once you get used to it.

NIJINSKY: Like you.

(NIJINSKY *kisses* ROMOLA. *They kiss and become passionate. He helps her out of her dress. He has her stand in her underclothes. They kiss again. He turns her gently around and kneels and caresses her buttocks softly and rests his head against her.* DIAGHELIFF *enters.*)

DIAGHELIFF: Have you forgotten, you're the god of dance? Get off your knees and get some rest, and for God's sake, make her shave her pubis!

(DIAGHELIFF *exits.* NIJINSKY *rises.*)

ROMOLA: What? But where are you going? Vaslav. Vaslav?

(NIJINSKY *is frightened. He starts to leave.*)

ROMOLA: Don't go. We must sleep together. Only people who fall asleep and wake up together really belong to each other.

NIJINSKY: (*Kisses her hand*) Forgive me. (*He exits.*)

(*End of Scene Three*)

Scene Four

(ROMOLA *is doing warm-up exercises in her room. She is in practice clothes. In another part of the stage is the rehearsal area. We see a barre and hear a piano offstage where an accompanist is playing Stravinsky.* NIJINSKY *paces.*)

(VASSILY *knocks on* ROMOLA's *door and when she answers motions for her to follow him.*)

VASSILY: Come!

ROMOLA: Where?

VASSILY: *Monsieur* Nijinsky. Practice.

ROMOLA: Rehearsal isn't for two hours!

VASSILY: Rehearsal, no. Class.

ROMOLA: He wants to see me dance?

(VASSILY *shrugs.*)

ROMOLA: Now?

VASSILY: Yes.

ROMOLA: *(Looks around wildly)* I can't.

VASSILY: Good. *(He smirks and leaves.)*

ROMOLA: Oh God!

(ROMOLA *runs after* VASSILY *crossing herself repeatedly. In the rehearsal room* VASSILY *enters and waits for* NIJINSKY *to finish.*)

NIJINSKY: No. What are you thinking? Stop! *(He paces.)* It's *presto prestissimo*. One and two and three and four five, one and two and three and four five. You're playing like you're dragging a dead horse. I can't believe you've played for the greatest dancers of the Ballets Russes. One and two and three and four five. Play it as Stravinsky wrote it. He is a musical genius, you are not!

(ROMOLA *enters, ready to greet* NIJINSKY. *He ignores her.*)

NIJINSKY: Enough! We have an opening tomorrow. Do you want to ruin everything?
Go practice where I can't hear you. *Prestissimo, prestissimo,* cretin! Go ahead. Go!

(VASSILY *is about to speak with* NIJINSKY *when the* BARON *pops in.*)

BARON: *(Popping in for a minute)* The girls are hysterical. We opened the trunks and the dresser packed only half the shoes. Arkady has a splinter in his foot and can't dance and all the doctors are at Mass. Oh, yes, they're sanding the stage floor so we can't possibly get in until four...which really means seven if we're lucky. It's a disaster. Why am I doing this? ...Sorry to bother you. *(He exits.)*

ROMOLA: *(Steps close to* NIJINSKY *and whispers)* You sent for me.

NIJINSKY: Vassily, come here. Please ask Toussia to come down in an hour. We'll practice our *pas de deux*.

VASSILY: I would like to watch this practice.

NIJINSKY: I don't care particularly what you would like this morning, Vassily.

VASSILY: Very good, sir. An hour then? Won't you need two or three— with her?!

NIJINSKY: Vassily! Go!

*(*VASSILY *bows and exits.)*

ROMOLA: He loathes me. He was the only person in the entire company who didn't come to our wedding.

NIJINSKY: Forget about it. It's nothing. We have an opening tomorrow. An opening is fate. It's everything. We win the audience. Or not. There are no second chances.
What was I thinking? I should have seen you dance sooner!

ROMOLA: You're speaking in Russian, Vaslav.

NIJINSKY: The dance needs precision, refinement. The slightest deviation, the smallest undue tension in the rhythm of the movement, any small mistake can destroy the whole composition. The dance becomes a caricature.

ROMOLA: Vaslav, I can't understand you.

NIJINSKY: I give class. Go to barre.

*(*ROMOLA *goes to the barre and does some stretches and pliés, loosening up.* EMILIA *and* DIAGHELIFF *enter.* DIAGHELIFF *is being very gallant. He bows and lets her enter first. He is in evening dress, and* EMILIA *is costumed as Medea.* NIJINSKY *moves over to watch* ROMOLA.*)*

NIJINSKY: *(Gently)* Close to fifth. Now! *Grande developpe en croix.* Leg up. Hold. Turn out. Turn out.

ROMOLA: My leg is already turned out.

NIJINSKY: No. Wrong. Must begin here. *(He adjusts her.)* Yes. Pelvis move forward and heel correct. Yes. There. Very good.

DIAGHELIFF: What did you expect? An artist to share your heart and soul? My poor Vaslav. Tsk, tsk, tsk.

EMILIA: She's quite good and quite beautiful.

DIAGHELIFF: *Madame*, she has no rhythm. A dancer without rhythm is a freak.

NIJINSKY: Arabesesque. Stretch. *Stretch*. Reach for rubies, diamonds, reach! Good. *(To* DIAGHELIFF.*)* You're jealous of my beautiful bride. Admit it, Sergei. *(To* ROMOLA*)* Now *cloche. Soutenus.* Feet together. Hold. Stay. *(To* DIAGHELIFF*)* You will be happy for me even though you can't love this way. She is brutal and sweet. Her eyes are blue green like the sea at Lido. Think of the Lido, Sergei, where you find all your beautiful little Italian boys stretched out on the beach, powdered with sand as if they are delectable blini covered with sugar. You will forgive me.

DIAGHELIFF: Never! You'll make babies, not ballets!

NIJINSKY: *(To* ROMOLA*) Plié* and *pique arabsesque.* Hold. *Paulement! Paulement!* Head like this—cheek rest on soft pillow. Again!

(ROMOLA *continues.*)

NIJINSKY: Too hard *Madame*. Not gorilla. Girl! Must be—light, light-stepping on eggs with no breaking. Again. No. No. Walk please.

ROMOLA: Walk?

NIJINSKY: Yes. Walk now.

ROMOLA: Have I done something wrong?

NIJINSKY: No. Walk, please. Away. Stop. Loose. Now walk. Not in *danse de style. (He takes first one hand and then the other and shakes it hard.)* Fingers close. Natural. *(He takes her hand again and shakes it harder.)* For beautiful hands, watch children. Children natural always. Walk. *Madame*, concentrate!

ROMOLA: *(To* EMILIA*)* Am I doing badly?

EMILIA: *(Staring at* DIAGHELIFF*)* Who wouldn't with all this faggotry!

DIAGHELIFF: *(To* EMILIA*)* Does he really know what it means to cross me? And to cross me like this? For a cow? I could almost cry for his ignorance. *(He turns his back.)*

NIJINSKY: Stop. You work too hard.

ROMOLA: You told me to work hard!

NIJINSKY: Dance not work. You are too tight. You move like cripple.

ROMOLA: I'm about to die from nerves. Of course I'm tight, but you can't understand because you're a machine, not a human being!

NIJINSKY: Dance never tight. *(He speaks in Russian out of frustration.)* Dance is simple. Like one breath and then another. Every step, every action is separate, but it must seem inevitable.

ROMOLA: Please speak French, Vaslav.

NIJINSKY: Ach! *(He walks away.)*

ROMOLA: Mother, what have I done?

EMILIA: Romuschka, I'm afraid for you.

ROMOLA: Don't say that. Why do you say that?

EMILIA: Look at him.

ROMOLA: He's an artist that's all and he's Russian!

EMILIA: Romola, his grandmother went mad and starved herself to death—

ROMOLA: So? Papa killed himself and I'm not insane.

EMILIA: He has a brother who sits drooling in a lunatic asylum.

ROMOLA: Stassik fell two stories and damaged his head. Everyone knows that.

EMILIA: You want to be his nursemaid the rest of your life. Is this what you aspire to?

ROMOLA: Why can't you just be happy for me and not state your cruel intentions as if they were prophecies? Everything will be splendid mother. I'd die for him!

EMILIA: One doesn't have to die for love, for love to be real.

ROMOLA: Papa did!

EMILIA: Enough! Enough! Your father didn't die for love. He died for greed. He embezzled money. It was a great scandal.

ROMOLA: You lie. You're lying.

EMILIA: And you can stop blaming me for your father's death. It wasn't I who placed a gun in his hand and made him blow his brains out. It was his so-called friends in Budapest who gave him the revolver and suggested that he end his life honorably.

ROMOLA: Why are you saying this?

EMILIA: To save you. Please. Leave Nijinsky...and if you are pregnant— have an abortion.

(EMILIA exits. ROMOLA goes to NIJINSKY.)

ROMOLA: What shall I do?

NIJINSKY: *(Not looking at her)* Dance. Dance. You may weep, but you must work. Even for the very back row of the *Corps de Ballet*. Dance. An artist must have one goal, one goal only—to perfect himself, to attain new heights in his art. Always, always.

(NIJINSKY *turns, hoping to be embraced by* DIAGHELIFF, *who stands back.*)

NIJINSKY: What have I done? What have I done? She is not a dancer. I've thrown my life away!

DIAGHELIFF: Good! Suffer! Die! I look at you and glass explodes in my heart. You want to puncture my heart and kill me? I can't endure this. I won't work with you. I can't work with you. I don't need you. There are stables full of young men. Academies! And, if they are not geniuses, they are beautiful and talented. The public will hardly know the difference. *(He exits.)*

(End of Scene Four)

Scene Five

(ANNA *is standing outside* NIJINSKY's *room. The* BARON *joins her.*)

BARON: Am I late? Well, it's no wonder. I've just discovered the world's greatest work of fiction —our contract with the theater! Nothing is true. Nothing! They promised us twenty musicians and we have five who speak God only knows what language. Yes, there are bathrooms, but none of them work and three dancers have diarrhea. I'm beginning to detest producing. It's debasing. Where is Romola and how are you, my dear?

ANNA: *(A little testy.)* I'm fine, Baron. Romola should be here any minute.

(The CAPTAIN *walks by rapidly with a suitcase that is far too heavy for him. The* MAN WITH THE PIPE *comes by arm in arm with an older, obviously wealthy woman who has a cane. They stop to confer together nearby. Both* BARON *and* ANNA *stare at them. The* MAN WITH THE PIPE *and the woman then stroll by. Neither gives* ANNA *nor* BARON *a glance.*)

ANNA: I hate the English.

BARON: Yes. Despicable.

ANNA: Do you know that man?

BARON: What man? Where? Which man?

ANNA: That man with the pipe.

BARON: Oh, no. Never met him.

ANNA: Don't bother. He's a sadist.

(ROMOLA *enters.*)

ROMOLA: Thank God you're here, Dimitri. I couldn't do this without you! *(Takes out a cigarette and lights it)* This will be my last cigarette.

BARON: Gracious, you sound like a condemned prisoner...

ANNA: I've left your bags. Do you need me for anything else?

ROMOLA: No. Thank you Anna....we might as well go in now.

BARON: Yes...but...

(ROMOLA *goes to put out the cigarette but* ANNA *takes it.*)

ANNA: Here, I'll take it.

(*Both the* BARON *and* ROMOLA *look at her in astonishment as she takes a puff.*)

ANNA: Ahh, camel dung! *(She exits.)*

(*The* BARON *and* ROMOLA *enter the honeymoon suite.* VASSILY *advises* NIJINSKY *of their arrival.* NIJINSKY *enters from the bedroom.*)

BARON: Vaslav, so good to see you. What a lovely suite. Oh, and a view from the harbor. My, my, doesn't that street down there remind you of that little section of Paris with all the strange shops. You know the one—where you can buy a new cranial saw or a wax model of a human nose complete with hair.

(NIJINSKY *isn't responding.*)

BARON: You did know I was coming?

NIJINSKY: *(To* ROMOLA*)* Why the Baron?

ROMOLA: Yes, well...there are some private things to say, but obviously, we must understand everything between us...so I've brought the Baron.

BARON: Yes, you see, she said that this is rather embarrassing, but...

NIJINSKY: Please, Dimitri. Don't insult me. I can look at her face and understand.

BARON: He says to continue.

ROMOLA: I'm nervous.

NIJINSKY: Tell her, she must talk without stopping. I am very nervous.

BARON: Vaslav asks that you speak freely.

ROMOLA: I can guess what he said. It's not so easy to speak as he supposes. *(She faces* NIJINSKY *directly.)* First, what did you think of my dancing? Will I ever dance like Pavlova, like Karsavina?

NIJINSKY: No, never.

BARON: Why not? She's very lithe and graceful.

NIJINSKY: *(To* ROMOLA*)* You begin too late.

ROMOLA: I understand.

NIJINSKY: But, I compose special little dances for you dance beautifully.

ROMOLA: Don't bother. I will never dance in public again.

NIJINSKY: That's stupid *(To* BARON*)* Tell her an artist can never...

ROMOLA: An artist what? I'm not an artist. God, I'm so sick of hearing this!

BARON: You have to go slower. He'll never understand you and he all but forbids me to translate! This is a disaster.

NIJINSKY: How can I love you if you are not an artist? An artist can traverse a whole world—by pacing from one wall of a room to the other. You see only four walls. A prison. I can't live like that! I asked you to learn to dance, because for me, dancing is the highest art. I wanted to teach you, but you became frightened. You didn't trust me. At that moment, I felt death. I had put myself in the hands of someone who could never comprehend me.

BARON: Vaslav wants you to dance.

NIJINSKY: Baron, *stop!*

ROMOLA: Then it's settled. You can't love me. We shall get an annulment!

BARON: This is impossible. I cannot be put in this situation! Vaslav, be reasonable. I must translate. These are very delicate matters. How will you understand each other?

(NIJINSKY *turns his back.*)

BARON: Romola Carlovna, what am I to do? Please I beg you—both of you—come to some agreement. Surely something can be done.

(ROMOLA *is silent.*)

BARON: And now what? What shall I do? What shall I tell Diagheliff? Oh yes, Sergei—or had you forgotten? I just wired him that you are married. He'll be in shock. He's most likely writhing on the floor in paroxysms of rage as we speak. Now he must be told something else? What?

NIJINSKY: Why don't we tell him about our intimate little dance company, Baron?

BARON: No,no no... That's impossible. He must not know me for the idiot that I am. I tell you I am haunted by stupidity. I scarcely have the character for my own relationships, let alone an entire company of them. I don't know how Sergei does it. *(He looks from one to the other. He shrugs.)* I suppose I shall have to ask him...if he is still speaking to me! *(He exits.)*

ROMOLA: Did you understand what I said? We haven't slept together. The Catholic Church will grant us an annulment.

NIJINSKY: Yes. I know this "annulment". I will do what God tells me. *(He closes his eyes.)*

ROMOLA: Do what your heart tells you.

(NIJINSKY moves toward ROMOLA and cups her cheek with his hand.)

NIJINSKY: Only God knows our heart.

ROMOLA: How can you think that, Vaslav? People don't love each other because of the love of God or the fear of God. We love someone because the world doesn't make sense if we don't.

NIJINSKY: Sense! What sense! *(He laughs softly.)* Roma, Romuschka, you are a dangerous girl for me. You have the willfulness of a rich girl. You live entitled, oblivious but you suffer. You love me and I am drawn to you with iron straps. Who knows what it is. You are innocent and wicked and brave. And you're beautiful. You are more beautiful than you are supposed to be. So beautiful that you should be stupid, but you're not stupid. I love you.

(NIJINSKY kisses ROMOLA. She kisses him. He holds her fiercely.)

ROMOLA: What is it, Vaslav?

NIJINSKY: You need words. I don't have them. I am a lullabyer. Rockabye, bye, bye, bye. Rockabye, bye, bye rockabye bye bye, rockabye bye bye. *(He continues hypnotized by his own words.)*

ROMOLA: Vaslav. Please.

(The dancers enter. The following dance should last about two minutes. As they dance—they encircle the couple in tighter and tighter circles and two of the dancers finally dance the couple offstage. The third dancer lays out a huge cross. The other two dancers come out with candles or small magical lights of some kind, genuflect and place them near the foot of the cross and exit. Other lights appear like eyes, some blinking, some staring, some human, some non-human.)

(End of Scene Five)

Scene Six

(EMILIA enters dressed soberly for winter. ROMOLA enters also dressed for a concert in winter. She carries an ornate chair and places it near center sage facing the audience. She retreats and waits—looking towards the wings. NIJINSKY stalks out angrily and sits in the chair staring challengingly at the audience.)

EMILIA: The second marriage, *le mariage avec dieu*. Who was invited? January 19th, 1919. A private recital. Saint Moritz Switzerland.

(EMILIA exits. ROMOLA is disturbed watching NIJINSKY. She darts apprehensive glances at the audience. She goes over to him.)

ROMOLA: Vaslav, please tell me what the pianist should play for you.

NIJINSKY: Quiet. Do not speak.

(ROMOLA *retreats*.)

NIJINSKY: I used to deceive my wife because I had too much semen. I had to ejaculate. I liked whores, but did not ejaculate into them. I have lots of semen and I keep it for another child. I hope I will be presented with the gift of a boy. God is a prick who breeds with one woman. I am a man who breeds children with one woman.
I used to give my wife roses that cost five francs a piece. I brought her roses every day—twenty, thirty at a time. I loved giving her white roses. Red roses frightened me. I loved her terribly, but already I felt death. My wife wept and wept.
She suffered. I wanted a simple life. I loved Tolstoy. I loved the dance. I wanted to work. I worked hard. I was like a draft horse, whipped until it fell to its knees and all its guts dropped out its ass. I lost heart. I noticed I wasn't liked. I weep and I weep. I love Tolstoy. I love Russia, although I am a Catholic Pole. I will work on a farm. I will practice masturbation and spiritualism. I will eat everyone I can get a hold of. I will stop at nothing. I will make love to my wife's mother and my child. I will weep, but I will do everything God commands me. *(A moment of sanity)* No! I do not love anyone. I am evil. I wish to harm everyone and be good to myself. I am an egoist. I am not God. I am a beast and a predator.

(ROMOLA *approaches cautiously, giving the audience anxious looks as if to invite their sympathy or understanding.*)

ROMOLA: Please, won't you begin *Sylphides*?

NIJINSKY: How dare you disturb me? I am not a machine. I will dance when I feel like it! *(To the audience)* You are stupid. You are beasts. You are meat. You are death. I feel God. I feel God. You came to be amused, but God wants to arouse you. I will dance frightening things. See? I can mimic a crazy person like my brother Stassik. I can be a whore, an old Jew with peyes, a cripple, an aristocrat. *(Looking around for the voices)* Who says workmen are good? Workmen are as depraved as aristocrats. They have less money. They drink cheap wine. My stomach is clean. I do not like meat. I saw how a calf was killed. I saw how a pig was killed. I saw it and felt their tears. I could not bear it.
See?
I can dance like a dying pig, like a dying Czar, like a soldier creeping in the shadow of the gate and shot— "unh" —in the snow. *(In his mind he hears a voice. he is joyful.)* Ay, I feel God. He loves me. I love him. Today... Today... Silence... *(He listens. He hears something, but it's not what he wants.)* Silence! Today is the day of my marriage with God!

(NIJINSKY *throws himself to the ground and makes fucking motions to the floor—a distortion of the ending of* L'Apres Midi. ROMOLA *covers her face.*)

END OF PLAY

THE SNOW QUEEN
A Fairytale For Strange Adults

THE SNOW QUEEN was originally produced at the Undermain Theater in Dallas, Texas, in December 2007. The cast and creative contributors were:

ANALIESE . . . . Anatasia Munoz
CHRISTIAN . . . . Christian Taylor
NINA IVERSON . . . . Shannon Kearns-Simmons
HENNER . . . . Matthew Posey
ERIK, PETER, BOY, PUPPETEER . . . . John Rawley
SIGRUN, GIRL . . . . Rhonda Boutté
HANS, MAID, PUPPETEER . . . . Kent Williams

Director . . . . Katherine Owens
Costume design . . . . Giva Taylor
Lighting design . . . . Steve Woods
Set design . . . . Linda Noland
Sound design & composition . . . . Bruce DuBose & Floyd Kearns-Simmons
Stage manager . . . . Mary Norman
Technical manager . . . . Ben Bryant
Assistant director . . . . Ruth Engel
Assistant stage manager . . . . Bianca Baidoo
Board operator . . . . Lynn Johnson

CHARACTERS

ANALIESE, *seventeen years old*
CHRISTIAN, *twenty years old*
NINA IVERSEN, *thirty-five to forty year old famous actress*
HENNER, *NINA's painter, companion*
JARL, *CHRISTIAN's friend*
PETER, *CHRISTIAN's friend*
ERIK, *lightly retarded fisherman's son*
YOUNG GIRL, *ten years old (an adult wearing a mask)*
YOUNG BOY, *spiritual warrior, ten to eleven years old (an adult wearing a mask)*
HANS, *spiritual warrior*
SIGRUN, *robber woman*

Some actors may play two parts.

Birds: a Toucan, a Peacock, a Swan, a flock of Geese, Seagulls, a Stork, a Falcon, and two Vultures. They can be shown in many ways: origami, Bunraku (shadow puppets), puppets, marionettes, gobo lights and so on...

ACT ONE

Scene One

(Two swings on opposite sides of the stage)

(Swing I:)

(Outside, rope swing with seat. CHRISTIAN *is pushing* ANALIESE *on a swing.)*

ANALIESE: Higher, higher...push me higher.

CHRISTIAN: Is that high enough?

ANALIESE: *(A happy shriek)* No...yes! Yes! ...I'm flying. Oh look Christian! Look at that beautiful light! Look at that light! Isn't it wonderful! Look at that sky!

(CHRISTIAN *pushes* ANALIESE *again, she shrieks and then laughs.)*

ANALIESE: Stop. Stop.

CHRISTIAN: You make me laugh!

ANALIESE: You make me laugh.

(They both laugh. They're having fun. It is the end of summer and we hear bird calls. Some Geese fly overhead. We hear the honking.)

ANALIESE: All those Geese. Look at them making a perfect "V". They're leaving.

CHRISTIAN: Well it is fall.

ANALIESE: Bye geese...good-bye. Good-bye.

CHRISTIAN: Don't tell me you're going to cry about it.

ANALIESE: Well it is an ending.

CHRISTIAN: They'll be back. They always are.

ANALIESE: Not all of them. Some of them die.

CHRISTIAN: That's true.

ANALIESE: Well say something.

CHRISTIAN: Keep your mouth closed when you look up at them or they'll shit right on your tongue! Birds are dirty animals.

ANALIESE: You're terrible!
Birds are beautiful, gorgeous animals and they stand on two legs just like us.

CHRISTIAN: Like us, please! An owl is like a cat with wings—it loves mice and pounces on them and it can hunt in the dark.

ANALIESE: Storks weep human tears when they're wounded.

CHRISTIAN: Who told you that?! Storks don't weep. They don't even speak or sing.
They only dance about and rattle their bills when they want attention. Don't be such a romantic.

ANALIESE: Why not? I love birds...like Meadowlarks! Meadowlarks sing while they fly. Other birds sing only when they're perched.

CHRISTIAN: Tiny birds. They're annoying. Most of them sweep in and out in huge flocks like swarms of flies. Give me a large bird! Like an Eagle or a Condor or a Falcon—then I could hunt grouse every day or climb mountains and cross rivers.

ANALIESE: Falcons! We could be falconers!

CHRISTIAN: We? We?

ANALIESE: Why not! I love Falcons. I see them every dawn riding the morning air, scouring the sky so they can look down and plummet on their prey like a lightning bolt.

CHRISTIAN: Gulping down your Meadowlarks.

ANALIESE: I love them anyway.

CHRISTIAN: Of course, my little Analiese.

ANALIESE: You think I'm stupid, that I don't know nature is savage?

CHRISTIAN: I don't think you're stupid. You're anything but. However I don't think you know about savagery and nature.

ANALIESE: And you do?

CHRISTIAN: I will. I'm a man. I'll be a sailor or a soldier, I'll be a hunter. I'll see my share of grief.

ANALIESE: I don't know what I'll see.
I wish I were a bird. I'd do exactly what I want all my life.

CHRISTIAN: Like what?

ANALIESE: Explore, wander—see Egypt and Turkey and Belgium and Africa.

CHRISTIAN: And you'd never come home?

ANALIESE: I'd always come home, but I'd be like the birds when they migrate...I would fly and fly and see the world, and then I could return home, to the place I started from. But it would all be different, you see—because I'd be different. I'd see it with fresh astonishment!

CHRISTIAN: Where do you get these thoughts? Sometimes you amaze me. Is there a hundred year-old person all curled up in this little head?

ANALIESE: You think I'm a child.

CHRISTIAN: No I don't.

ANALIESE: You treat me like one. What I wonder though, is If you think I'm such a child—why are you always with me?

(CHRISTIAN *stops the swing and kisses* ANALIESE *on the mouth.*)

ANALIESE: Oh!

(ANALIESE *hugs* CHRISTIAN.)

CHRISTIAN: Damn! I shouldn't have done that. You'll take it too seriously. *(He exits.)*

ANALIESE: I love you with a thousand hearts.

(End of Scene One)

Scene Two

(19th Century cabaret/nightclub)

(We focus on swing two:)

(Swing two:)

(A nightclub spotlight. A red-haired singer in a long flowy but tight pink chiffon gown singing on a swing which is hanging from a thick branch. White roses rain down on her as she sings. People applaud and whistle. A group of young boys clap and stamp. Among them is CHRISTIAN! *She sings with a fake French accent.)*

NINA: Mock the devil
And he will flee
Mock the devil
And set me free.
Come on baby
Look at me.
You want the fruit
Come shake the tree.

I am waltzing with the devil
On a spinning rope.
Cut me down
Give me hope

You can do it
You can do it
You can do it
You can do it
You can...

If you—
Mock the devil
He will flee
Come on by
And rescue me.
You want the fruit, baby
Just shake the tree.....

(NINA *jumps off the swing and bows to the audience who is chanting her name.* HENNER *helps her off the swing.*)

HENNER: Fabulous. Fabulous. Nina. As always. Will you marry me? (*She laughs and throws kisses.*)

NINA: Aren't I Venus rising from the silver spray?

HENNER: You never answer me.

NINA: Because it just means you're feeling lonely—and your loneliness is greater than your fear of bondage...at the moment.

HENNER: That's not true.

NINA: Have I made you fall from grace?

HENNER: Yes.

NINA: Do I make the earth move?

HENNER: Always.

NINA: Then I can not take your question seriously.

HENNER: Why not.

NINA: Because obviously you haven't learned the difference between wanting to spend the rest of your life with someone and wanting to experience continuous moments of ecstasy!

HENNER: Oh Lord!

(*End of Scene Two*)

Scene Three

(An aviary in Copenhagen, 1892. Large tropical plants in pots. Birds on branches. A Peacock, a Toucan, a Stork. Bird calls. Sunlight. CHRISTIAN *and* ANALIESE *enter.)*

ANALIESE: The Aviary. What they said is true. It's like a jungle.

(Small birds are circling around.)

ANALIESE: The plants have leaves as big as my face.

CHRISTIAN: Look there's a...a Toucan. See the sign!

ANALIESE: Yes! A Toucan. Black as a Raven but a beak like a boat! and there's a Peacock prancing with her cape and crown like a princess...

*(*NINA *and* HENNER *enter.)*

CHRISTIAN: Like a prince. It's a male—only the males have all the adornments...

ANALIESE: You're wrong. There's a Peacock and she's a woman! That's Nina Iverson the actress. She's adorned.

*(*NINA *sees* CHRISTIAN *and* ANALIESE *staring at her and she blithely waves to then.)*

NINA: Henner—applaud the Danes. They've almost equaled the Belgians with this aviary.
It is small but green and airy. I love it.

HENNER: And here I am. Domesticated nature puzzles and bores me.

ANALIESE: You *have* noticed Nina Iverson, the actress?

CHRISTIAN: I believe so yes.

ANALIESE: I don't know why everyone is so enthralled with her. She looks old. At least forty-five.

NINA: *(Reading a sign on the cage.)* A Toucan—from Central America. Do you miss the jungle my pretty one? Flying freely in the treetops with your monkey friends chattering about? Oh and a Peacock from India with a thousand eyes on its tail—Are you friends? Born continents apart—but with the same dank climate. I have no patience with the tropics. They all make me think of rotting leaves and leper colonies. Plus they have no Winter. No, no, no no. I must be in the north. I have a hunger for it— the brilliance of ice, the silence of snow. All peace and glory. Am I not a snow queen?

(PETER *and* JARL *enter, friends of* CHRISTIAN. *They wear their winter hats and gloves and coats which are open. They are rude and wild and run around opening the birds' cages....*)

PETER: Freedom! Freedom.

JARL: Don't be an ass. They might escape. They'll die in the cold!

PETER: You call being in a cage living?

ANALIESE: They call it home! (*She goes after the birds, extending a branch and trying to get them back in their cages.*)

JARL: So Christian, you coming sledding or not? We've been waiting for hours!

PETER: You missed seeing Jarl acting like an idiot.

JARL: I was not.

PETER: Was too. Stupid bugger almost got killed. Hitched his sled to a monstrously fast sleigh and was whipped under its runners.

JARL: I skidded out again.

PETER: So are you coming or will your little "wife" get mad?

NINA: *(To* HENNER*)* Little wife...

CHRISTIAN: She's hardly my wife. She's a baby.

ANALIESE: I'm not a baby and you don't have to babysit! Go off and make a fool of yourself. It's quite a job being a man, isn't it? One insult or a snigger and you're off to break a bone or shatter your skull to prove how manly you are.

JARL: And what do little girls do—cry?!

CHRISTIAN: Don't cry, you make your nose all red and ugly!

ANALIESE: Just leave.

JARL: Come on Chris.

CHRISTIAN: *(To* ANALIESE*)* You are alright, aren't you?

PETER: Come on. I can't stand such tender good-byes.

JARL: Hurry. The square will be deserted. There'll be no sleighs at all.

(*They start out.* CHRISTIAN *looks back at* ANALIESE *who ignores him. He brushes into* NINA.)

CHRISTIAN: I'm sorry. I'm so sorry. How clumsy of me.

NINA: Not clumsy. I doubt you have a clumsy bone in your body. But hurried? Rude? Yes.

CHRISTIAN: I apologize.

NINA: Oh shit, Henner.

CHRISTIAN: Excuse me?

NINA: *(To* HENNER*)* We've found someone with good manners!

HENNER: You're impossible.

NINA: I hope so...

CHRISTIAN: Well...

NINA: You don't know what to say, do you?

(CHRISTIAN *looks nervously—first at* ANALIESE *who turns her back and then at his friends who are watching him amazed.)*

NINA: Are those your friends?

CHRISTIAN: Yes. They are.

NINA: Well then, give your friends a thrill. Tie your sled to my sleigh. I'll take you to the square or wherever you want. I have four of the fastest horses you've ever seen, given to me by a sheik from Arabia. What do you say? Do you dare?

CHRISTIAN: Dare?

NINA: Yes. Dare to come with me. *(To* HENNER*)* He's hesitating. *(To* CHRISTIAN*)* Are you afraid?

CHRISTIAN: No. Of course not. I'll try anything—especially if I'm dared!

NINA: Anything?

CHRISTIAN: I do exactly what I please with my life.

NINA: I do too. We'll meet by the gate then.

CHRISTIAN: By the gate. Of course. By the gate. Madame, Sir. *(He bows and starts to leave passing his friends.)*

HENNER: Must you?

NINA: Must I what?

HENNER: Indulge your irrational passion for novelty?

NINA: Look at him, Henner. He's beautiful. He's a love.
Don't you love young people Henner? They'll do anything. They are such works in progress.

(NINA *and* HENNER *exit.)*

JARL: Oooo-la la. "The gate"! And you even smell like Miss Iverson. If I close my eyes, I might kiss you!

CHRISTIAN: *(To* ANALIESE*)* You see I must take care of these half-wits. They obviously can't do a thing without me!

JARL: Half-wits? You cretin.

(The young men exit. The aviary birds are circling and calling out.)

ANALIESE: Don't let the birds out! Nit-wits. All of you. *(She tries unsuccessfully to keep the birds in the aviary.)* Don't fly away! Don't fly away! If you get away, what if you're not free? What if you're lost?!

(End of Scene Three)

Scene Four

(By a pier. We see the rowboat with a long rope pulled tightly to something offstage. We hear ocean and Gulls swipe around. A large young man is throwing stones at them. ANALIESE *walks up with a backpack.)*

ANALIESE: Hey you! You! Don't kill those birds!

*(*ERIK *pays no attention. Keeps throwing stones)*

ANALIESE: Stop!

ERIK: I can't. I must get that one. See? It's a Raven. A Raven means death!

ANALIESE: It's not a Raven. *(Astounded)* It's a Toucan!

ERIK: Toucan? Is that Finnish for Raven?

ANALIESE: No it's a tropical bird.

ERIK: I don't care what it's called.

ANALIESE: Oh never mind. It's survived. My God, it's kept warm a whole winter.

ERIK: Ach! Whatever it's name. It is dark and has a big beak. It is the devil. If it is the devil then I must kill it or it will shriek and ride my back until I go mad like my Grandpa Urs. The devil descends shrieking on his back and flogs him. Then Grandpa tells me the only place to hide is in the bottom of a bottle. But if Grandpa Urs drinks his bottle to the bottom, he flogs me. So I must kill this devil. Now you made me lose him. Oh no! Oh no!

ANALIESE: Oh no! He flew away. I've lost him.

ERIK: He's gone. This time I was lucky. I can tell you that.

ANALIESE: Sir, boy, tell me. Where am I exactly?

ERIK: Are you stupid? You're on the beach.

ANALIESE: I know. But what beach?

ERIK: This beach. Why do you want to know?

ANALIESE: I'm looking for someone.

ERIK: Here?

ANALIESE: I don't know.

ERIK: Well I can take you all the way to Odense. Grandpa Urs is a ferryboat man.
When he dies I get his boat. He's not really my grandpa. My father's head was cracked under a wheel.

ANALIESE: I see.

ERIK: My mother didn't want me because I'm simple. She gave me away. Grandpa Urs likes me cuz I'm his eyes now. He can barely see. He's old. He has his ferryboat sixty eight years. I been going... *(He laboriously counts his fingers)* ...six years. Wait! *(He pulls a lump of chocolate wrapped in a handkerchief out of his pocket and begins to eat it.)* Chocolate.

ANALIESE: Grandpa Urs must be very good to you if he gives you chocolate.

ERIK: Grandpa Urs? Ha! The beautiful red-haired lady who sings gives me chocolate.

ANALIESE: A beautiful red-haired lady?

ERIK: Yes. And her boyfriend. Every winter she takes her boyfriend to her ice palace. Every Spring she comes back alone.

ANALIESE: But the boyfriend must come back too if she takes him again the next winter!

ERIK: Are you stupid? It is not the *same* boyfriend!

ANALIESE: But...?

ERIK: If I eat one bite of chocolate every day, I can make it last to... *(He hands the handkerchief with the chocolate to* ANALIESE.*)* ...If I don't eat any more...
to *(Count on his fingers)* next month. Six months.

ANALIESE: So you saw them six months ago?

ERIK: Five, next month will be six. I can count pretty good. Next November I will get more chocolate because I am bigger and I can push the others away.

ANALIESE: Why would you push them? Why not just ask?

ERIK: No. Did you ever see a walrus? They smell like a pig. One tried to tipple our boat. *(Taps his head)* I threw some fish as far as I could from the boat and the walrus went after it. Next year—when the red-haired lady comes with her boyfriend and throws chocolates from her boat—I'll grab them all and throw some far away so the other boys go off after them, just like the walrus.

ANALIESE: That's very smart.

ERIK: Yeah. Give me back my chocolate. *(He takes it.)* Yeah when the red-haired lady comes. She's rich. She goes all the way to...to...Skagen.

ANALIESE: How do you know she goes to Skagen? Did she tell you?

ERIK: I don't talk to her! I don't know the woman. This time I talk to her boyfriend. He ran to the boat and knocked me down, then picked me up and cleaned my face with a handkerchief. He said they were going to Skagen. He was tall. He gave me his handkerchief. See? I got my chocolate in it. *(He unwraps his chocolate.)*

ANALIESE: What a beautiful handkerchief. It has initials. Look—a "C".

ERIK: Yes. A "C" and a "P".

ANALIESE: Let me see it?

ERIK: No.

ANALIESE: But I like it.

ERIK: I like it more. *(He stuffs it away.)*

ANALIESE: You say the young man went to Skagen? With the woman?

ERIK: She's a woman and then some. Grandpa Urs says her hair is the color of the Danish flag.

ANALIESE: Red.

ERIK: Sure. He said he'd salute her anytime.

ANALIESE: And the young man looked healthy and alive?

ERIK: Of course.
How could he give me his hankerchief if he was dead?

ANALIESE: Does your Grandpa Urs take his boat to Skagen?

ERIK: We go to Jutland. To...to Glatvid Strand for the seals. The sea's too big at Skagen. Maybe if you had a lot of money Grandpa Urs would take you up a river.

ANALIESE: I have no money.

ERIK: Then Grandpa Urs will take you nowhere.

ANALIESE: Could you help me? You could sneak me onboard.

ERIK: I don't know. Grandpa Urs would hit me. I'm bigger, but I let him hit me. I scream though.

ANALIESE: You're smart. Hide me.

ERIK: I don't know...

ANALIESE: All right then. We'll play a game. Like hide and seek. I will hide where Grandpa Urs will never find me.

ERIK: Oh sure. You want to play. But I can't hide. I have to work. *(Whispers)* Sometimes I hide.

ANALIESE: Yes?

ERIK: I hide in the little boat. See? The life boat, there. You could hide there too.

ANALIESE: I suppose so.

ERIK: He never goes there. And you know what else? I'll walk next to you until you get in. Grandpa Urs will just think it is me walking alone. His eyes are bad.

ANALIESE: Thank you. But never mind. *(She starts to leave.)*

ERIK: Are you stupid? Where are you going? The boat is right here.

ANALIESE: The crossing is cold and wet. I would freeze.

ERIK: That's true.

ANALIESE: I would die.

ERIK: That's true.
Oh!
I know. I'll put some sheep with you and cover the top. Their bodies are warm and their shit is hot!!

ANALIESE: What if lightning strikes or the waves drown me?

ERIK: You decide. Come or don't come. There's nothing I can do to stop the sky or the ocean from doing what it will do. So?

ANALIESE: I'm coming.

ERIK: Ach! Let's go then.

(They start off.)

ERIK: Oh no! Wait!

ANALIESE: What?!

ERIK: My name is Erik. Erik Blid.

(They exit.)

(End of Scene Four)

Scene Five

(Centerstage. Balcony. Peacock pacing. Huge double French doors. Dance music. Intermittently we see a couple dressed formally, sweep by behind the doors. We hear loud Peacock cries. All of a sudden HENNER bursts through with a Lady. They are slightly drunk. The Lady takes off her shoes. They linger for a moment. Giggling, heads close together. Perhaps one of them carries a glass of Champagne. They move into a corner.)

(NINA bursts in. She has an orchid in her hair. She is fanning herself. She looks over at HENNER, smiles to herself and moves to another part of the balcony. The Peacock goes to her. HENNER notices NINA and whispers something funny into the woman's ear and she tries to put her shoes back on. She can't which makes her and HENNER laugh louder. The Lady exits, waving and throwing kisses as she re-enters the dance.)

HENNER: Women!

NINA: Are you being successful?

HENNER: I shouldn't be, but I am!
How horrible!

NINA: Why?

HENNER: Well they are nothing but...

NINA: But...? Describe them, silly! Women are nothing but—

HENNER: A knife in the heart.

NINA: Oh rubbish. Is that how you would describe me?

HENNER: You? You.

NINA: Yes.

HENNER: You want the truth?

NINA: Will it hurt?

HENNER: Yes.

NINA: Well say it—I'm ugly. I'm untalented.

HENNER: No none of that.

NINA: Then go on, describe me.

HENNER: You're a woman fifteen years older than you want to be.

(Long pause)

NINA: Go away. You're drunk and disgusting.

(CHRISTIAN *enters, bright and excited, carrying glasses of Champagne.*)

HENNER: True. Well...back to the *Totentanz*. (*He exits.*)

CHRISTIAN: (*To* HENNER) What is "*Totentanz*"?

NINA: It's German for "the dance of death", my dear.

CHRISTIAN: What a gloomy old man.

NINA: He's got his demons. I suppose we all do.

CHRISTIAN: Well they haven't found me yet.

(*They toast each other.*)

CHRISTIAN: I pray they never find you. (*He kisses her.*) I'm immensely happy. Tremendously impressed! I can't believe all this...

NINA: What? Civilization?

CHRISTIAN: Oh please—you know exactly what I mean. I mean, here we are...the two of us. And any idiot can see that at least ten or twenty men want to dance with you or take you church and immediately to bed... and they all have much more to offer you.

NINA: Don't be ridiculous.

CHRISTIAN: Ridiculous?! There are two men there with titles.

NINA: Yes. "Pervert" and "priss".

CHRISTIAN: Another is a famous surgeon, another owns fleets of ships and three villas in Greece—which he continuously likes to mention...

NINA: And you?

CHRISTIAN: I...I...think you're the most beautiful woman I've ever seen. There! Do I sound like every other man you've ever met?

NINA: No.

CHRISTIAN: No?

NINA: The men I've met have said it hundreds of times to hundreds of women. I doubt you've ever said that before.

CHRISTIAN: No I haven't.

NINA: Ahhhhhhh—look at you. You're blushing!

CHRISTIAN: I am not.

NINA: How adorable.

(CHRISTIAN *puts his arms around* NINA's *waist and lifts her in a whirl as part of a dance.*)

NINA: You're so sweet. So sweet. I want you never to go away!

CHRISTIAN: Is that true? Do you mean it? I've heard other...

(NINA *kisses* CHRISTIAN *to stop him from talking.*)

NINA: Don't listen to other people, especially about me. They know nothing. My world is a world of secrets. Sometimes my friends try to protect those secrets with lies.

CHRISTIAN: I hate lies.

NINA: What about secrets?

CHRISTIAN: Hmmmm secrets...not so bad. In fact they're sort of like frontiers. Yes, they offer the thrill of the unknown, like the ocean and whales.
I have an idea—let's follow the whales!
I think I saw one. It was as big as a barn.

NINA: You want to go hunting whales?

CHRISTIAN: Yes.

NINA: You've gone from love to whales? Unbelievable. You're such a boy.

CHRISTIAN: Why? Because I like to hunt? You like to hunt. You like to master things and conquer them.

NINA: Yes I do. But I don't often want to kill them. And why whales? They don't interest me in the least! They lead such obscure and exemplary lives—quite unlike actresses.

CHRISTIAN: They speak. Did you know? Their voices sound like wind in a cave.

NINA: I could never kill a whale. Why are we talking about whales?

CHRISTIAN: I don't know.

NINA: I don't know either.

CHRISTIAN: There are other things to talk about.

NINA: And do.

(NINA *puts his arm around* CHRISTIAN.)

CHRISTIAN: An act of love?

NINA: Yes.

CHRISTIAN: Now?

NINA: Why not?!
Don't you want to?

CHRISTIAN: More than anything!

NINA: Good!

CHRISTIAN: Great!

NINA: Let's dance!

CHRISTIAN: What?

NINA: Dance. You know, one, two, three—one, two, three. La la laa-la, la la laa-la.
While seducing a woman, you should always dance.

CHRISTIAN: But....

NINA: Dancing is the vertical expression of a horizontal desire which will come later....

CHRISTIAN: Dancing?

NINA: *(Laughing)* Dancing is lovely. I love the feeling of your hand in the small of my back. My cheek on your shoulders.
When we're dancing, everything between us seems easy. So easy. Love most of all.
Now don't pout.

CHRISTIAN: I can't help it. I was expecting....

NINA: Shhhhhh my love. There is still so much to learn about each other. And if you learn only one thing from me. Remember—never expect anything ever, not from any god or any person!
We all live in the moment.
Now please me.

CHRISTIAN: How?

NINA: We'll dance. I love to dance.
Then I'll please you.

(NINA *takes the orchid out of her hair and slides it between his teeth. They glide through the doors and dance.*)

(End of Scene Five)

Scene Six

(ANALIESE *climbs out of the rowboat and is tugging it on shore. There are Swans. A young* GIRL *runs out wildly and starts to spin. The Swans honk and take off. We see their shadows over the group and then they disappear. A young* BOY *also stumbles in. Both children are played by adults wearing child masks.*)

ANALIESE: Girl. Girl. Come help me with this boat.

GIRL: *(Twirling.)* I can't. I'm a lily. I'm a lily. I'm a tiger lily. *(She growls and falls to the ground.)*

ANALIESE: You're spoiled. That's what you are.

(The GIRL *doesn't get up.* ANALIESE *approaches her.)*

ANALIESE: Girl, are you all right?

GIRL: Listen to the drum—boom, boom!

ANALIESE: Look at you half—naked and there's still snow on the ground. Who let you go out like this?

(The GIRL *moans.)*

ANALIESE: Are you all right? Should I call your mother?

GIRL: There are only two notes—boom, boom. Hark, the women's dirge. Hark, the cry of priests. The Hindu woman stands on the funeral pyre in her long red robe; the flames fly up around her and her dead husband. But the Hindu woman is thinking of the living man there in the crowd whose eyes burn hotter than the flames that will soon burn her body to ashes!

ANALIESE: You're delirious. Where do you live? What can I do?

(The BOY *stumbles close and suddenly sits staring vacantly.)*

ANALIESE: Boy! You there! *(She starts towards him.)*

GIRL: Hot! Can the heart's flame perish in the flames of the pyre?

*(*ANALIESE *goes back to the* GIRL. *Afraid to leave her)*

ANALIESE: You there, boy. Can you help me get this girl home?

(The GIRL *falls asleep.)*

ANALIESE: Wake up. You can't sleep. If you sleep in the snow, you'll die. *(She goes to the* BOY.*)* Boy! Boy!

BOY: Leave me alone.

*(*BOY *also sleeps. A large Stork flutters down and tries to wake him.)*

ANALIESE: No. Wake up! What is the matter with you two? Are you drunk? Are you poisoned?

BOY: I only speak my own story. I am a Stork.

ANALIESE: You are mad.

BOY: *(Grabs her wrists harshly)* I know the pond where all little human babies lie till the Storks fetch them and give them to their parents.

(The Stork flaps away slowly.)

BOY: Now we shall fly to the pond and fetch a little brother for the boy who threw stones at us.

ANALIESE: *(Frees herself and looks around desperately for help)* Of course we shall.

BOY: Yes.

ANALIESE: Why don't I take you home?

BOY: No! We'll go to the pond.

ANALIESE: It makes no sense to go to the pond. If the boy threw stones and was bad and wicked—why bring him a baby?

BOY: In the pond is a little dead baby—it has dreamed itself to death. We'll take it to the boy and he'll cry because we have brought him a little dead brother.

(HANS, a young man runs in.)

HANS: There you are you wicked children! Scaring me to death. I shan't read to you ever again! ...Oh! hey. Who are you?

ANALIESE: Analiese. What's wrong with the children?

HANS: No time to explain. Give me a hand with the girl. I'll take the boy. Follow me!

(They drag the children across the stage a large thatched roof appears over them. We see the reflection of flames from a fire. HANS exits and brings back two blankets. He throws one to ANALIESE and they tuck the children in.)

ANALIESE: What's you're name?

HANS: Hans. Thank you. Please sit down I'll bring some tea. Do you like tea? I make special tea. We have some bread too. *(He brings out a tray with tea and bread.)*

ANALIESE: What's wrong with the children? Hans: Oh yes. You wouldn't know. So Sorry. I'm exhausted. They shouldn't leave me with young children. You see how naughty the children have been.
And I'm the one responsible for them now. I'll be in a lot of trouble.

ANALIESE: What's the matter with them?

HANS: I...well I gave them some poppy seeds and read them from Hans Christian Anderson—which they seemed quite enamored of. They were quoting him to you and quite well, don't you think? But I think I over did it with the poppy seeds. I put some in your tea too. Well they aren't really poppy seeds but they do come from a poppy. A little opium never hurt anyone—see, the little minx are fine now. But it looks like you aren't. There's blood on your hands and you're clothes are ripped! Here let me clean them for you.

ANALIESE: Thank you. It's nice and warm here and I'm so tired. May I stay a moment?

HANS: A moment? Stay for a week or a year. There's only sixty of us here. No one my age. And no young girls! And you're pretty. So pretty I've lost my breath at least ten times since I've seen you. Who would have thought that the gender of my own mother would cause me so much delight! So stay as long as you want!

ANALIESE: You are so funny.

HANS: Am I? But thoughtless. You must want something more to eat and drink.

ANALIESE: Well yes, yes I'm hungry and thirsty. My insides have turned to dust! So thirsty.

(HANS *brings tea.*)

ANALIESE: It's very nice here. Rustic. Are the children your brother and sister? Where's your family?

HANS: Yes, well...Analiese. You said your name is Analiese, am I correct?

ANALIESE: Yes?

HANS: We need to talk before the Elders come back.

ANALIESE: The Elders?

HANS: Yes. You see—to live here you must be part of this spiritual community. And all are adults, the Elders, except the two wee ones and well, me. We consider ourselves spiritual warriors foraging for a pure life in the woods. We call ourselves the "New Vikings" —although we're not the "let's heave rocks and eat brains" variety. And no human sacrifices. Absolutely not! Just the occasional bird or horse. In fact, the Elders are down the river offering horse entrails to Loki as we speak. Loki is a very tricky fellow—especially near springtime when he deserves a lot of attention.

ANALIESE: I'm afraid I don't know who Loki is.

HANS: The river god. I suppose you're a Christian.

ANALIESE: Yes certainly.

HANS: We were too. Once. However, now we're true Northmen. We worship the old gods—you must have heard of Thor or Odin, who hung upside down for nine nights from the Tree of the World until he could see the future.

ANALIESE: You don't believe in one God?

HANS: The White Christ? Hardly. We're animists with some modern adjustments. You must want to eat now. Have the soup. I'm a tolerable cook, but a dreadful hunter.

ANALIESE: Aren't you afraid you'll go to Hell if you're not Christian?

HANS: You mean that place where bad people go to suffer and scream forever? No. No no. We have much more majestic ideas. We've bridged the idea that, on the one hand, God took some dirt and shaped us in his image. You do know that as a Christian, no matter how good-looking you are, you're nothing but glorified dirt?
Anyway, we've bridged that idea with the idea that God has breathed life into us so the essence of God is in us. In Christianity those two halves don't fit. How can you be dirt and God? The Vikings were right in the first place. You can be dirt and God if God is everything—the white birch, the squirrel, the poplar, the sun, the river. To us the whole natural world is sacred. And we act accordingly...most of the time.

ANALIESE: I like the way you talk.

HANS: You do? How do I talk?

ANALIESE: Beautifully and complicated.

HANS: Really?
I haven't had much practice. It's all been in my head.

ANALIESE: You should be a poet.

HANS: Thank you. That's very kind. I hope to be one. I've read so many poets. I read a tremendous amount. The Elders brought books with them. Hundreds. But I think I've read them all four times by now. My head is full of useful topics—Hindu rituals, the discovery of Africa, the proper construction of meat-drying racks. I read to the children to keep them from going mad.

ANALIESE: The children. I'd nearly forgot. You must be worried about them.

(HANS *goes to check them.*)

HANS: No they're all right.

ANALIESE: Are they your brother and sister?

HANS: No. No relation.

ANALIESE: And there's no one your age?

HANS: No such luck. So actually it's quite nice we stumbled into each other.

ANALIESE: Yes it is. I think you saved my life.

HANS: And you mine. You're my only friend now.
But look at you—you need bandages, you need clothes. *(He brings out a pile of things.)* Look, look! Take whatever you want!

ANALIESE: But the Elders!

HANS: We are generous people. Here. This would look good. And this. Let me bind your hands. Are they burnt from the oars?

ANALIESE: Yes.

HANS: Let me help you. Don't be shy. Bodies are natural things.

(HANS *helps* ANALIESE *clean and change.*)

HANS: You are beautiful. Not that beauty matters that much—after all the Elders say, "if only the most beautiful birds could sing, all the woods would be a silent place".

(*Small flocks of Sparrows and Gulls swoop through, calling out.* ANALIESE *and* HANS *kiss.*)

ANALIESE: Some more hot tea.

HANS: Yes. Yes. You need more tea. I'll put some flower extract in it for you.

ANALIESE: What flower extract?

HANS: The Brits call it Opium. They bring it from India. It's quite nice I've taken it to stop my head from throbbing. We're only supposed to use it during ceremonies. It can be quite powerful when you take a lot. We use them to contact our spiritual guid s from the past. The Vikings appear to us in dreams and explain their myths. But don't worry. I won't misjudge the amount for you as I did for the children. There.

(HANS *and* ANALIESE *clink cups. He kisses her again.*)

ANALIESE: I shouldn't be kissing you—but I don't care!

HANS: Good!
Now I don't miss the other lad.

ANALIESE: What lad?

HANS: My other friend. Well, almost. There was one young man who passed through here last November who looked promising. He came through with a gorgeous red-haired woman dripping in diamonds and fur. But I believe their party was drinking too much...I don't think that was a dream...and drove their horses over the rocks into the river that crushed them and dragged their bones out to the sea.

ANALIESE: What did you say? That they died?

HANS: I'm not sure.

ANALIESE: Didn't you check to see if they were wounded and could be saved?

HANS: Well, you see, the Elders went. I mean someone has to stay with the children!

ANALIESE: You said this lad was your friend—is this the concern you show for your friends?

HANS: Well he was *almost* my friend. I didn't really know him, but I wanted him to be my friend.

ANALIESE: You were asleep weren't you. You'd taken opium!
Oh my God, it was Christian! He's dead and gone!

HANS: Yes the red-haired woman and the lad are gone. Gone. At least I think they are. I believe that's how the Elders obtained the horse entrails we kept to sacrifice to Loki this week.

ANALIESE: If I follow the river I'll find them.

HANS: You'll reach the sea. That's all! It happened months ago.
Nothing could be left.
Stay here, Analiese. Why would you want to leave?

ANALIESE: I love that lad.

HANS: Stay and save me.

ANALIESE: Hans, I can't save you.

HANS: Please.

ANALIESE: Save you from what?

HANS: I will dream myself to death! Analiese please. I need your help. I think I am getting worse. I gave the children opium to keep them quiet while I was dreaming, such gorgeous dreams of color and music. They almost make it bearable here. But I gave the children opium. Too much and they wandered off. What if they had fallen asleep and a wild animal tore them apart? What if they walked into the water and drowned?
The worst is I think I would do anything to anyone to keep dreaming.
Analiese please stay. You must!

ANALIESE: Don't tell me what to do!

HANS: I have given you Opium. You will not get far. And I will follow.
(*He falls asleep.*)

(ANALIESE *scrambles up and packs some things and runs out the door. She starts to stumble and then kneels.*)

ANALIESE: Christian. I don't know where you are now or if you're anywhere—but I must find you. The world is empty with you gone. No...no...not gone...you can't be. I can still see you, I can still feel the exact weight and warmth of your head on my lap. I can still smell your hair and see the clarity of your eyes. You can't be dead. You will never die in me. I promise you. I swear. And if you drowned, if you did, when I go to my grave, we will be together. I don't know how that's done. But this time, I know that when you reach out, your hands will not find water, they will find me. (*She falls asleep. It snows.*)

END OF ACT ONE

ACT TWO

Scene Seven

(A flock of Geese flies by. We hear the honking and see the rush of their wings as they fly in clean harmonious triangles. CHRISTIAN *and* NINA *pause to look at them.* NINA *has been reciting lines from the play* Miss Julie *and* CHRISTIAN *has been reading his character from another book.)*

CHRISTIAN: Can it be almost Spring?

NINA: Why?

CHRISTIAN: The Geese are returning. They remind me.

NINA: Of what?

CHRISTIAN: Of other Springs.

NINA: That it's time to return to your little friends?

CHRISTIAN: No

NINA: Then what?

CHRISTIAN: Nothing.

NINA: Tell me. You can tell me anything.

CHRISTIAN: Can I?

NINA: We talk all the time.

CHRISTIAN: I thought we only talk when we cry out to each other in bed at night.

NINA: We're talking now. What is it you want? Tell me. I'd love to give it to you.

CHRISTIAN: I want you to know me. I want to know you.

NINA: That takes time, my love.

CHRISTIAN: How much time?

NINA: One never knows. It's different with each person.

CHRISTIAN: Is it?

NINA: What?

CHRISTIAN: Different with each person? ...Or does each boy have his season?

NINA: I don't know what you're referring to.

CHRISTIAN: Don't lie. I hate lies. I may be young, but I'm not stupid. I watch you. I walk through the rooms and I hear things. The servants say you bring a young man here every winter and you "educate" him and then desert him.

NINA: The servants are crass and they say ugly things. We're beautiful together. We're delicious together. We help each other. I can't tell you how much help you've been in reading *Miss Julie* with me. And you're so patient with my nerves. *(She paces.)* We haven't seen a *Miss Julie* in Denmark for nine years. I must make the part mine. She must be imperious and yet vulnerable.

CHRISTIAN: I can't believe I'm any help at all. I get so caught up with you that I lose my place.

NINA: You're reading well. Even Strindberg would be proud. You could almost be an actor...but don't even think of it. The last thing I need is another actor. I need a man like you, who will understand emotion and feel it as a matter of interior experience rather than as an opportunity for dramatic display.

CHRISTIAN: Are actresses very much like actors then?

NINA: Enough talking! Let's go on to the next scene *(She turns the pages for him.)* All right, you're reading Jean, the servant. His girlfriend is asleep in the other room.

CHRISTIAN: We're here?

NINA: Yes. I shall begin. *(As Miss Julie)* A charming wife she'll make. Does she snore too?

CHRISTIAN: *(As Jean)* She doesn't do that, but she talks in her sleep.

NINA: How does Jean know Christine talks in her sleep?

CHRISTIAN: He's heard her.

NINA: So you know what is going on there, don't you?

CHRISTIAN: What?

NINA: Here where it says they look at each other. There is an understanding between Julie and Jean.

CHRISTIAN: Yes, that he sleeps with his girlfriend.

NINA: But Julie is there anyway.

CHRISTIAN: Yes.

NINA: So there appears to be an understanding.

CHRISTIAN: Yes.

NINA: Good. Let's go on then. From the look... *(As Miss Julie)* Why don't you sit?

CHRISTIAN: *(As Jean)* I wouldn't permit myself to do that in your presence.

NINA: *(As Miss Julie)* But if I order you to?

CHRISTIAN: *(As Jean)* Then I shall obey.

NINA: *(As Miss Julie)* Sit then. No, wait. Can you give me something to drink first?

CHRISTIAN: *(As Jean)* I don't know what we have in the icebox. Only beer, I think.

NINA: *(As Miss Julie)* What do you mean, only beer? My taste is very simple...

CHRISTIAN: Simple? I doubt it!

NINA: *(Repeats loudly as Miss Julie)* My taste is very simple. I prefer beer to wine.

(CHRISTIAN *laughs at* NINA.)

NINA: Don't be snide. Try to do the actions as they're written. Hand me a beer.

(CHRISTIAN *mimes giving* NINA *a beer.*)

NINA: *(As Miss Julie)* Thank you, won't you have one yourself?

CHRISTIAN: *(As Jean)* I'm not much of a drinker, but if Madam orders me-

NINA: *(As Miss Julie)* Orders? Surely you know a gentleman should never allow a lady to drink alone.

CHRISTIAN: *(As Jean)* That's perfectly true. *(He mimes opening a beer.)*

NINA: *(As Miss Julie)* Drink to my health now! *(As* NINA*)* Hesitate a minute. There. *(As Miss Julie)* Are you shy?

CHRISTIAN: *(As Jean)* To my Mistress's health!

NINA: *(As Miss Julie)* Bravo! Now kiss my shoe and the ceremony is complete.

(CHRISTIAN *starts to do so and pulls back.*)

NINA: Christian, do as it says.

(CHRISTIAN *looks at* NINA *then removes her shoe and brings his lips to her foot, then kisses her ankle and her calf. He raises his head and looks at her.*)

NINA: Christian, that's not...

CHRISTIAN: I know.

NINA: *(Withdraws her foot and puts on her shoe)* You've quite gotten into the role.

CHRISTIAN: The role is me, I think, and you.

NINA: You're hardly a servant.

CHRISTIAN: But you're playing with me in all sorts of ways, and I understand them all. *(He stands and puts his arms around her.)* Just like in the play.

NINA: I suppose we must talk. Sit.

CHRISTIAN: Am I Jean then? Is that an order?

NINA: Don't be silly.

CHRISTIAN: Nina listen— Oh God, we share a bed but I feel I should still be calling you Miss Iverson. I don't know you, but I love you. I feel like a wheel of fire is rolling through my chest.

NINA: Don't say wild things like that—you could make me truly fall in love with you.

CHRISTIAN: You? The snow queen would let herself melt? I doubt it.

NINA: Fine then! I should send you back home. You can sit under your cuckoo clock with your mother and father and eat meatballs and gravy!

CHRISTIAN: No

NINA: Why not?!

CHRISTIAN: This is too new, too strong. I need you with me, close to me a little longer.

NINA: Then don't pout.

CHRISTIAN: Forget it!

NINA: The mood's spoiled, isn't it. But it will come back. At least for a while. Trust me. I understand. Sometimes the real world gets too big for us and we have to find a way to try and match it. I do it as a romantic idealist. Do you know what that means?
I take lovers.
I believe with each new lover I can reinvent myself and dispose of the troublesome person I've become—just like a snake shedding its skin. You may need to do that too.

CHRISTIAN: I need some air.

NINA: Go on, leave. I'm cross as well!

(CHRISTIAN exits.)

(End of Scene Seven)

Scene Eight

(Opium dream)

(ANALIESE is lying on the back of a Swan. Snow comes down around her. She is dreaming. On the other side of the stage, NINA, totally in white, shakes a metal sheet that makes noise like thunder. When the thunder ends, NINA turns her back and walks away into the snowfall. CHRISTIAN appears and takes out a lump of coal from his pocket and colors the area around both eyes black and marks black across his mouth. He stares out at the audience and also disappears into the snow.)

ANALIESE: Did you hear that sound? Is it thunder? I hear thunder but there's not a cloud in the sky. Thor is the God of Thunder, isn't he? I wonder if Hans is praying to him somewhere. I wonder if it does him any good. He should repulse me. He should repulse me. How cruel to put opium in my tea. I had terrible nightmares. In one, Christian and I were children making peepholes in the frosted windows with heated pennies we pressed against the glass. There was a great snowstorm—the snow fell faster and faster and the flakes were enormous. One became a woman dressed in white lace made up of millions of tiny star-shaped flakes that cut you when you touched them. She was so pretty. She was made of ice but she was alive! Her eyes glittered, but there was no peace in them. She nodded to us. Christian was wild to open the window. I couldn't stop him and he went out. When he turned to wave, his nose and fingers were black with cold. Does that mean he's really dead? Oh I should hate Hans, but I can't!

(ANALIESE falls asleep with her arm around the Swan. We hear Crows cawing and see the shadows of many flying around. Two Vultures enter one on the shoulder of a lone figure, SIGRUN, who carries a large bundle. The other Vulture lands near ANALIESE and the Swan takes off. SIGRUN approaches ANALIESE. She pulls out a long silver knife and sniffs around. SIGRUN now and then tries to wave off the Vultures, but they circle and land again. They are hard to get rid of.)

SIGRUN: Flowers! No. Ahhhhhh.... Girl. Pretty, pretty, pretty. *(She opens her bundle and pulls out two sticks of wood; crosses them and reacts as if they have become a lighted fire. She sighs; takes off her jacket of skins and warms her hands and her butt. She pulls a lump of food out and cuts it with her knife. She is comfortable, takes a bite. She sniffs ANALIESE again.)* Yep. Smell. Like flowers. *(She gives ANALIESE a light kick.)* Hey you! *(She squats examining ANALIESE from head to toe. Lifts her head by the hair and lets it drop.)* Still soft. I shall have a playmate. *(Takes a blanket out of her bundle and wraps ANALIESE and puts her in a sitting position and shakes her a little.)* Wake up! *(Puts her knife close to ANALIESE's face.)* Oooooo! Good . Best knife. Poor Russians. *(Watches some more)* Look, her little paws are twitching like a dog's when dreaming. *(She tickles ANALIESE's chin with her knife.)* Girl...oh girl. Hey!

ANALIESE: Hans! Don't touch me! Get away!

SIGRUN: *(Startled. Leaps back)* I leave you to die ripped apart by wild animals!

ANALIESE: Oh God. Are you the only one here?

SIGRUN: Yep.

ANALIESE: Who are you?

SIGRUN: No names. Not mine. Not yours. I hate to know stranger's name. It makes me sad. What if I have to kill you and you have a name? Like killing a pet. Too sad.

(ANALIESE *is shaking violently, recovering from the cold.* SIGRUN *goes in her pack and pulls out some raw meat and sticks it on the end of her knife.)*

SIGRUN: You need food. *(She holds the meat over the two sticks as if cooking.)*

ANALIESE: What is that?

SIGRUN: Stag liver. Lucky. I gutted deer this morning. So, you one of those Viking people? *(She laughs heartily.)*

ANALIESE: Why are you laughing?

SIGRUN: Tell me first. You one of them?

ANALIESE: No. You know them?

SIGRUN: Yep. Sure. I trade with them. With this! *(She holds up her knife.)* Violence is my currency—like gold or bread. I trade them their life for anything they carry. They don't carry much. I don't bother them. Ummmmm—maybe sometimes for fun; when they do their ceremonies... especially ones with *blackfly* dance. *(She jumps from side to side, slapping at invisible flies and pretending to scratch bites on her arms and legs.)* Big, strong Vikings! They dream they're great warriors, but they're weak, puny—live in their heads. Puh! They believe throwing stones into river makes it rain. That is stupid.
Throw stones into deep part of river. Drive fish downstream into net. Now that is smart. I do that. *(She spits.)* You sure you not one of them?

ANALIESE: No!

SIGRUN: *(Holds out meat)* Here. Fresh kill. Have you killed?

ANALIESE: No!

SIGRUN: Not a little fish. Not a little mouse? Not once?

ANALIESE: Never!

SIGRUN: You will. Someone, something will die because of you.

ANALIESE: Don't say that! Why do you say that?!

SIGRUN: I see it. Everywhere. Children left during famine, dying along the road. Their mouths green from eating grass; deserts so dry you slit your horse's belly to suck water from its stomach.
Death. Yep...Too many.
What you doing here?

ANALIESE: I'm looking for a friend...yes, a friend. He might have gone up north to the Ice Palace, or maybe he died on his way there. You might have seen him pass months ago in a big sleigh covered in ropes of silver with gold bells and six horses with braided tails and...and with a woman.

SIGRUN: A beautiful woman?

ANALIESE: Yes. Yes. That's the one!

SIGRUN: Of course.

ANALIESE: Then you saw him.

SIGRUN: No.

ANALIESE: But you knew about the woman...

SIGRUN: Obvious. Always so. *(Laughs loudly)*

ANALIESE: *(Slaps SIGRUN's face.)* Don't laugh at me! Don't you dare laugh at me!
I have traveled hundreds of miles. My feet are freezing, my hands bleed every night, my heart is breaking.
I don't know if this man is alive or dead, and I must know.
Now! Now!
I will find out and you will help me!
So stop laughing!

SIGRUN: *(Immediately serious...for a moment.)* You are right. One does not laugh about love. It is serious. There are no jokes about love.
About sex....well, everyone laugh about sex. I know many jokes. I not tell them. You not my friend. *(She grabs ANALIESE and hugs her, still holding the knife.)* We still have fun. You come with me. I get you good Russian boots. We go rob the Finns. We become rich. I show you sights you never dreamed. Bones of whales and polar bears—so big—they lie around like legs and arms of giants! Maybe... Maaaybe then we friends. I'll see.

(HANS *enters wrapped in a blanket.*)

ANALIESE: Hans!

SIGRUN: He bother you? *(She moves close to him with her knife drawn.)*
Hello Viking boy.

HANS: Don't interfere Sigrun. I've handled you before.

SIGRUN: Then there were three. Now you're alone.

HANS: *(To* ANALIESE*)* I must talk to you. I must apologize.

ANALIESE: *(To* SIGRUN*)* Help me

HANS: Talk to me! All night I've been fighting angels. They float outside my window.
Some had silver wings and gave me good advice; "See Analiese; apologize, be good". But there were bad angels with bloody wings and scowls. They say if I talk to you, I'll die. But I've come anyway because you are worth my life. I must talk to you.

SIGRUN: No

ANALIESE: Go away Hans. I have nothing to say to you.

HANS: You must let me explain.

SIGRUN: Give me your blanket and you can talk to girl.

(HANS *shoves it at* SIGRUN.)

SIGRUN: Nice blanket. *(She lays it on the ground and sits watching the two of them as if it were a cock fight.)*

ANALIESE: There's something wrong with you. You gave me opium. You could have killed me. Just like the children.

HANS: I never would have left you in the snow. I was coming for you. The Elders arrived. I had to wait. But tell me—did you see things when you slept?

ANALIESE: Terrible things.

HANS: You saw the power of opium?

ANALIESE: Yes I did.

HANS: You could lead me away from it, Analiese. You have that power for me.

ANALIESE: If I do have that power, it's one I never wanted and one I don't understand.

(HANS *approaches.* ANALIESE *backs away.* SIGRUN *is enjoying this.*)

HANS: Don't back away. I stopped. See? I would never harm you. But that boy you love. He didn't deserve you. Look how much he's made you suffer; forcing you to travel alone and unprotected through the wilderness.

ANALIESE: He didn't force me. I already told you. I chose to.

HANS: I don't believe you. Love doesn't choose. It happens. It has happened to me.

ANALIESE: Hans.

HANS: With you. You see? You've made me a poet. I wrote you a poem.
It's my first. *(He is trembling with cold and emotion.)* I loved once but not again.
Blindly, sullenly completely.
I loved a girl not yet a woman.
Green-eyed as drunk as I was
with golden skin and arms that smelled
of woods and grass and ached for something
as liquid and eternal as love..."

ANALIESE: Hans, just go back to your home. You frighten me.

HANS: Is that all you can say, Analiese?

ANALIESE: Save the poem. It's wonderful. But give it to someone who can love you back. I never can.

(ANALIESE *tries to return the poem.* HANS *won't take it. So she drops it.*)

HANS: *(To* SIGRUN*)* She thinks she's in love with a dead man. But I know better. *(To* ANALIESE*)* I know you have deep feelings for me. *(He tries to embrace her.)*

(SIGRUN *steps in.*)

SIGRUN: Are you deaf or crazy? She said she didn't want you.

(HANS *looks at her knife, weighing whether he should fight* SIGRUN *or not. He resigns himself to the moment.*)

HANS: *(To* ANALIESE*)* This girl is not your friend.

SIGRUN: Yes I am. I've decided. Shall I let him go or kill him?

ANALIESE: Don't harm him. Please. He'll leave. *(To* HANS*)* If you love me as you say you do, you will leave.

HANS: All right. *(Backing away)* You see? I'm gone. I've passed your first test. *(As he is leaving)* But I will see you again, Analiese. *(He exits.)*

SIGRUN: *(She picks up* HANS' *poem. Looks off in direction he left. Crumples paper)* If you live.

ANALIESE: You can't kill him.

SIGRUN: Life is big surprise.
Death is even bigger surprise.

ANALIESE: I must go on. You understand?

SIGRUN: No.

ANALIESE: It's love.

SIGRUN: Money better. Money like wings, carries you above danger and hard times.

ANALIESE: I'm going anyway. I can't stay here!

(ANALIESE *takes her things and runs off.* SIGRUN *calls after her.*)

SIGRUN: My name is Sigrun. You are Analiese. We are friends. No mistake. You will see.

(SIGRUN *follows* HANS. *She follows him slowly at first. Crows circle wildly and caw. The Vultures leave. She finds him. She runs after him. Her knife is drawn.*)

SIGRUN: I know you follow her.

(SIGRUN *stabs* HANS. *He falls with a grunt and is still. She drags him away.*)

SIGRUN: Viking's loved the sea. Go then. In only this you a Viking.
The ocean will be your grave.

(End of Scene Eight)

Scene Nine

(ANALIESE *is in her boat. Geese and Cranes take off from shore, making their calls and flying around her a while and then leave. Gradually the sky is filled with flights and calls of Seagulls.*)

ANALIESE: I smell the open ocean. Yes there it is—the open ocean...and the waves...the waves that can sweep away the sand, or topple buildings and flood the streets. This is the ocean. This is the ocean. *(She jumps out of her boat and pulls it until she feels it is secure. She runs around.)* Imagine I have ridden the back of this river all the way to the ocean, right where the land starts and ends!!
But I've never found the sleigh with Christian's bones. What is that?
Oh, the prow of a ship shattered on the rocks. And there? What is this that passes? A swimmer?

(HANS *with black around his eyes and covering his lips walks slowly across the stage, passes the boat.*

ANALIESE: Hullloooooo. It's a fish. See he has a silver fin. No look. It's a boy. He has a dagger stuck in his back. He's pitching over. Hans! Hans! Oh he's been killed.

(ANALIESE *tries to reach out for* HANS, *pulls out the dagger and he exits.*)

ANALIESE: This is Sigrun's dagger. What has she done?!

(CHRISTIAN *stands on a rock with a great hooded Falcon on his arm.* HENNER *stands nearby.*)

HENNER: Now my boy, we always fly Falcons at first light. Thus we avoid attacks by golden Eagles—see there on every knoll and outcrop.

There and there—all those giant raptors, those gargoyles black against the dawn sky. Those are Eagles. They won't fly until the late morning thermals blow in that put them effortlessly into the heights.

CHRISTIAN: So now the hunt is safe. We can free our Falcons to fly.

HENNER: *(He removes the hood.)* Yes, but remember, a Falcon is free to become independent every time it's flown—and they often do leave.
The trick to keeping a Falcon is not to take freedom away from the bird, but rather to get the bird to see the advantages of the relationship with the falconer.

(NINA *on a large plush chair holding a mirror. A young* MAID *servant is brushing her hair.)*

NINA: Oh God. I feel my age.

MAID: I know what you mean. My mother never looks at herself in the open sunlight.

NINA: I'm not old, you stupid girl! I'm tired.

(NINA *slaps the* MAID *who starts to run out.)*

NINA: Oh Lord. Don't be such a ninny. Come back and brush my hair.

(The MAID *comes back and continues to brush* NINA's *hair.)*

NINA: I'm devoting time to feeling sorry for myself. I'm so tired these days.

MAID: That's what young men do to you.

NINA: Not physically tired. Oh what would you know? I'm tired. I'm tired of love.
No, not of love, of love affairs so short that love is offered, consumed and spit out. Oh God, I'm tired of two people lurching away like drunkards from the mess they've made. This time I'll take my turn at living, just once, this passion, this madness, this infatuation to the very end. It would be too terrible for him to leave my body now—especially since it will probably never happen again.

(End of Scene Nine)

Scene Ten

(NINA *is sitting for a portrait. The Toucan from the aviary is at her shoulder. A Peacock walks back and forth.* HENNER *sketches rapidly on a large notebook.)*

HENNER: Turn a little to the left. Yes. And lift your chin.

NINA: *(To the Toucan)* Don't bite me Monsieur—you little devil. I saved your life.

HENNER: Perfect.

NINA: Not if he bites my nose. No he never bites me. Do you, Monsieur? You love me.

HENNER: *(He sketches.)* Do you want tendrils around your face or something more severe?

(NINA *is preoccupied, she doesn't answer.*)

HENNER: Miss Iversen.

NINA: What? Oh—sketch one of each. I'll want several portraits to last the tour.

HENNER: You have many admirers.

(*A flock of Geese fly by honking, calling to each other. The Peacock at her knees cries out.*)

NINA: That may be, but these are for patrons. Admirers must pay their own painters if they want a portrait.

HENNER: Keep your chin up so your face is towards the light.

NINA: Like this?

HENNER: Yes. If you could only bring yourself to smile.

NINA: Wasn't I smiling?

HENNER: No you looked rather sad.

NINA: The Geese are flying North.

HENNER: So?

NINA: Well I don't like it.

HENNER: It happens every Spring.

NINA: I hate Spring! So much moving around, airing out, scrubbing—

HENNER: Spring. The changing of the guard.

NINA: Not this year.

HENNER: No?

NINA: I am considering a promotion not a discharge.

HENNER: Please.

NINA: I'm capable of change. Christian will stay.

HENNER: And you're telling me because....?

NINA: This time is very different for me.

HENNER: Really?

NINA: Yes, Henner.

HENNER: Oh.

NINA: Don't be sad, you silly man.

HENNER: Me sad? No.

NINA: We all change. Well, don't we? Come on. You're no longer in love with me are you?

HENNER: I know better than that.

NINA: Then don't be sad because of me. Be sad because you hate Spring!

HENNER: How can I hate Spring?
By next week, the sun will shine. I will be painting Mister Moritz's daughter on the beach. It will be quite lively. One of his musicians, an American dwarf named Billy, will play the violin while Mister Moritz shoots ducks. I will be very happy.

NINA: Aren't you finished yet?

HENNER: Don't move. We're at the most crucial point.

(*Two* SERVANTS *enter half carrying, half dragging a very tired, wild-looking* ANALIESE. *They put her down.*)

SERVANT 1: We found her wandering on the beach.

SERVANT 2: Yes. On the beach.

SERVANT 1: I said that.

SERVANT 2: Well, I can say it too. Her name is Analiese. That's all she'll say.

SERVANT 1: (*Slap's the other's head*) I was going to say that!

SERVANT 2: Well you didn't, did you?

NINA: Boys!

(*As they exit.*)

SERVANT 1: You better be nice to me.

SERVANT 2: Or?

SERVANT 1: Live by the sword, die by the sword!

SERVANT 2: Reap what you sow! (*Offstage*)

SERVANT 1: An eye for an eye!

HENNER: Analiese.

ANALIESE: (*Approaches the Toucan*) So she's taken you too!

NINA: Be careful. He bites.
He's beautiful, isn't he? I saved him. He would have frozen. He mistook escape for freedom. *(To the Toucan)* Didn't you, darling?

(HENNER is circling ANALIESE.)

HENNER: She's not from around here. Where the hell did she come from. Eh? I'd like to paint her, just as she is. So wild, dirty, animalistic. *(He goes to touch her face.)*

ANALIESE: Get away, you dog!

HENNER: She was going to bite me, that little tart!

NINA: I'd watch out, Henner. Perhaps she's feral. Who are you, girl?

ANALIESE: You don't remember?

NINA: No. Should I?

ANALIESE: I suppose you were only looking at Christian.
But I know who you are.
Yes. You're an actress and a thief!
(She takes out her knife.)
I want to see Christian now!
Where is he? Christian Pyndt!
He was on his sled and went with you.
Seven months ago. Seven months and six days since we met at the aviary in Copenhagen. Don't you remember me?

NINA: Not at all.

HENNER: Yes you do. She was the one the boys were referring to as Christian's "little wife"?
You laughed.

ANALIESE: Forget me, laugh at me—just tell me where Christian is.
He left and never came back.
I was told he was dead. Has he died? Is he dead?

HENNER: Shall I take her knife?

NINA: No. She won't use it.

ANALIESE: Of course I'll use it. I've seen it done by a woman who split a deer carcass and then killed a man with the same knife. Do you think that left me untouched?

HENNER: Nina...

NINA: Leave her alone, Henner. She won't use it—that poor, poor girl.

ANALIESE: Why? Why am I a "poor girl"? Is Christian dead? I heard he was dead. Is he dead?

NINA: *(Snatches the knife away)* Only to you. *(Flashing the knife)* See Henner? I do know what I'm doing. *(To* ANALIESE*)* To me Christian is very much alive.

ANALIESE: Alive and breathing?

NINA: Yes of course. I saw him just the other day.

ANALIESE: Thank God. Thank God. Thank God.

NINA: Well of course God rules us all and it is His grace and style to let us live as He pleases, but then again, He has given me a major role in providing for Christian. After all, we have lived together and fallen much in love these last seven months.

HENNER: Nina....

NINA: Well this poor girl has made a tortuous journey. She has shown the courage of an explorer, so she deserves to know what her expedition has found.

ANALIESE: *(She runs around shouting.)* Christian! Christian! Christian! Christian! Christian!! *(She sinks to her knees.)*

NINA: Christian has gone falconing. He'll return in a week.

ANALIESE: I see.

NINA: You won't need this. *(She returns the knife to* ANALIESE*)* I am sorry. Truly. You have done such a stunningly envious thing—your journey, your love. But you must understand. all you have done is for naught. The past is the past. It's over. It's gone.
All that all-embracing love took place on borrowed time. The past. That time has run out. Poof! Blown away like ash in the wind. Gone.

ANALIESE: It's not gone. Not for me. The only home I've had all these months has been my feelings for him.

NINA: I'm sorry.

ANALIESE: I don't believe he's fallen for you. You don't know the first thing about who and what Christian is or what he needs. You were nowhere near the site of his happiness and his memories. But I was there. I am a part of him.

NINA: Childhood memories are not sacred. Your Christian has gradually and gently allowed those memories to fall apart in favor of different landscapes offered by another woman. In fact he's dropped your memory like a stone down a well.

ANALIESE: I don't believe you! How would you know? After a few months you think you know what he wants?

NINA: Yes. I absolutely do.

ANALIESE: What?

NINA: Not what you want. Not little bourgeois dreams and illusions.
Not a wife, or a warm hearth or a weekly beer draught with his pot-bellied little tinker-buddies. He's seen a bit of the world and he hungers for more.

ANALIESE: So do I.

NINA: So do I.

ANALIESE: So?

NINA: So, now we will do our little *Totentanz*.....

ANALIESE: What's that?

NINA: Our dance to the death. Our finale.
Our competition for Christian.
I can't believe I'm doing it.
It's disgusting. This self-betrayal of women for a man has always struck me as a dire mistake. But here we are, waiting for man to form our life.
Oh God, the times I've seen this in others, dreaming of romance. Some of them go mad, some are deserted for a young girl. Ditched. You can hear the word hit them, hear the sound of the blow.
Love makes one capable of immense stupidity. I hate it!

ANALIESE: Well I hate it too.

(The Peacock lets out a scream. We faintly hear the honking approach of a flock of Geese.)

NINA: *(To the Peacock)* Do you want to be free, my little prince? *Mais, non, non, Non*...you would be gobbled up in a minute in this mad, mad world. All your jeweled ornaments would be picked away by grudgy little creatures—we can't have that.

(The honking of Geese and flapping of wings grows louder as a "V" of migrating Geese pass. ANALIESE *runs to look at them.)*

ANALIESE: I love the Geese.
You know what, Miss Iverson?
I'm not waiting!

NINA: What?

ANALIESE: I would like to pack some food and leave. I am not waiting.

NINA: You're giving up? Just like that?
Unbelievable. I'm almost disappointed. I thought this would be a real test of our mettle and our heart.

ANALIESE: I, for one, don't need any more tests of character. I have proven myself. I have fought to come here and won. I have found that Christian is alive. Thank God. But to sit here and wait for Christian with you? All we'll

have for each other are questions. A relationship of questions. What kind of beast is that?!
I have traveled so far on so little to find him. That gives him his answer about me.
And I am not here to watch him weigh and scramble about for answers. If he wants me, he'll search for me.
So tell Christian I am following the Geese on their migration. I have learned so much from birds. I have watched how wild birds skim through the wild world and learn from their wild experiences but still return home.
So tell Christian I understand now that home is a destination not a starting place.
Tell him, if he's smart, he will become more like birds and less like those humans who find each other, lie with them in the dark and then lose them again. Geese mate for life.

NINA: You are leaving.

ANALIESE: Oh yes. I'm off to Finland. I have a friend there. I must tell her I have found her knife.

NINA: How will you know if I tell Christian you were here?

ANALIESE: I will only know when I see him again. But I know you will tell him, because you want the answer to my questions as much as I do.

NINA: Good, go then. There's food in the kitchen. I'll even give you a horse for your foolishness.

(ANALIESE *exits.* NINA *cries.*)

HENNER: You've won. Why are you crying?

NINA: I don't know.

HENNER: What are you feeling?

NINA: I don't know.

HENNER: You really must learn to put a name on your emotions. It makes them manageable—for you and for other people!

NINA: You must help me up. I fear my whole leg is cramped from sitting too long.

(HENNER *helps* NINA *up. She leans against him.*)

HENNER: Are you afraid?

NINA: I'm the Snow Queen.

HENNER: What do you think will happen when you tell Christian that Analiese has come all the way from Copenhagen to find him?

NINA: Let's take a walk along the beach, Henner. I love the ocean. The ocean is one of three things that make life worth living.

(*As they exit*)

HENNER: And pray—what are the other two?

NINA: (*Leaning on his arm*) Hospitality and revenge.

(*End of Scene Ten*)

Scene Eleven

(*It is night.* HENNER, *in a robe, sits at a table with a lantern, some cheese and some wine.* CHRISTIAN *enters just putting on his night robe. They startle each other.*)

CHRISTIAN: Henner!

(HENNER *starts to choke.*)

CHRISTIAN: Easy man. Are you all right?

(HENNER *nods.*)

CHRISTIAN: What are you doing up so late?

HENNER: Eating away my sorrows. Would you like some?

CHRISTIAN: Sorrows? No. Not really. (*He pours some wine.*) Cheers!

HENNER: Welcome back! How was it?

CHRISTIAN: It was fantastic! What I always dreamed of— A land of Eagles and Hawks and nasty Owls who will split the head off a goose like cracking ice. I took my Falcon to the edge of a cliff, a glacier, and I stood there thinking about how the wind may have blown for thousands and thousands of miles not touching anything else before it touched my face.

HENNER: But you're glad to be back?

CHRISTIAN: Why yes.

HENNER: Still?

CHRISTIAN: Of course. What has changed?

HENNER: Hasn't Nina told you?

CHRISTIAN: Told me what? She told me she missed me, she loved me. I can still smell her on my skin.
What else do I need?

HENNER: So she didn't tell you?

CHRISTIAN: About what?

(The Peacock enters. HENNER *drops some crumbs for it.)*

HENNER: Nothing.

*(*NINA *stands in the doorway.* CHRISTIAN *doesn't yet see her.* HENNER *does.)*

CHRISTIAN: Stop being so annoying Henner. You know you have something to say. Say it!
Be a man.

HENNER: Did Nina tell you about Analiese coming here?

CHRISTIAN: Christ! Analiese?

HENNER: Analiese from Copenhagen. You do remember Analiese?

CHRISTIAN: Of course I remember her! What was she doing here? Was she all right? Did she come alone?

NINA: She was here alone. Our boys found her last week. Brown, dazed and scratched and thin—desperate, I'd say. Looking for you. She was wild as a wolflet.

CHRISTIAN: You saw her?

NINA: We spoke for quite a while.

CHRISTIAN: And you never told me.
Well God, I want to see her. Where is she?

NINA: She left the same day. She had some friend in Finland. She was following the Geese migration.

CHRISTIAN: You never said a word.

NINA: I forgot. I didn't think it was important.

HENNER: She's lying. The girl specifically pleaded with her to tell you.

CHRISTIAN: *(To* NINA*)* You bitch! *(To* HENNER*)* How was she?

HENNER: At first the poor girl was all confusion and suffering after the mess wrought by her journey. Then...

NINA: Henner!

CHRISTIAN: You betrayed me!

NINA: Why? Because someone you never mentioned to me dropped in? Because I spared her the pain of having sacrificed so much and then seeing you in love with another woman? Please! If there was any betraying, it was done by you. You betrayed her the moment you left her in anguish without a word so many months ago. What did you think—out of sight, out of mind? You left her as if she would simply turn into a statue that you could bring back to life whenever you wanted, like in a fairy tale. Even I think she deserves more. After we spoke, she realized that and she left. I didn't make her leave.

CHRISTIAN: But you didn't tell me about her sacrifice, that she'd come all this way.
Analiese—with her little pale triangle of a face and delicate bones like a bird's. I swear you could hold her up against a candle and count them with your finger. She came all that way, for me.

NINA: You're upset.

CHRISTIAN: Upset? I'm furious!

NINA: Why? Because you didn't see her or because she didn't wait to see you? What did you think —that she would weep for a thousand years and never forsake her lost love?
Anyway, I thought you would never want to see her again.

CHRISTIAN: What? What do you mean you thought we'd never see each other again?

NINA: You left her without a word. You never said a word about her to me.

CHRISTIAN: Because I felt terrible about the way I treated her. Where did she go?

NINA: Do you love her?

CHRISTIAN: Yes.

NINA: Would you leave me for her?

CHRISTIAN: Yes.
I would leave you, a woman who can betray me, a woman who can't love a man -only a boy whose life she can create.

NINA: That's enough!

CHRISTIAN: Which way did she leave? Tell me.

NINA: No.

CHRISTIAN: What kind of woman are you?

NINA: If you love her. Find her. The way she found you. Henner. You caused all this! Talk to him. Help him leave. I refuse to deal with him any longer. Winter is over. His year is up. *(She exits.)*

CHRISTIAN: Henner?

HENNER: Yes. Yes. I'll show you exactly where she went. Let's go.
Oh Lord, look, it's almost morning. The sun is rising.
The snow in the moonlight was so beautiful, wasn't it?
It's almost sad to watch the moon fall.

(End of Scene Eleven)

Scene Twelve

(HENNER and NINA by the sea under a red moon. Seagulls cry in the distance. An Owl circles. The Peacock and Toucan walking a ways away and then exit.)

HENNER: You almost had me believing you were in love.

NINA: Please, I never stop acting. I love acting. I'm always acting, always, always and everywhere. When I'm asking the time, ordering breakfast, making love—it's all acting, endlessly acting, eternally touring. You should know that by now.

HENNER: With Christian, you gave me a fright.

NINA: Did I?

HENNER: Yes, especially when you didn't ask why I told him about Analiese. I admit it was a betrayal—but I couldn't help myself.

NINA: Of course not—falconer that you are. You always feed your bird the heart when it makes a kill.

HENNER: You do love him. *(Silence)* Do you hate me now?

NINA: No.

HENNER: But you will have a new young friend?

NINA: I don't think I want any more young friends. Older men are much more grateful.

HENNER: Are we?

NINA: Look, an Owl.

(The Owl comes out and flies in silhouette against the moon.)

HENNER: I wish we weren't so different.

NINA: Not so different, my darling Henner. The monogamist and the promiscuous are quite alike when it comes to love. Both are deluded by hope.

HENNER: You make me cry.

NINA: Do I?
Don't cry over me.

HENNER: I cry for you.

(The wind blows, the waves hurl in.)

NINA: Oh Henner, Get me a shawl.

(HENNER *exits.*)

NINA: *(Singing)* When you've woken at midnight
All tangled and cold
You've looked in the mirror
And seen your grey soul
Seems your life's over
But your story's untold
I'll be your voice in the dark.

If you're looking for trouble
Cause that's all you've known
If you harvest the whirlwind
Cause that's all that you've sown
If it seems like you'll never, ever find home.
I'll be your voice in the dark.

A voice in the wilderness
A cry in the night
Deep eyes of a women
You can't get behind
Who's lost too much love
To be silly or kind
I am your voice in the dark.

(The Owl flies up and covers the moon. The stage is dark.)

END OF PLAY

SELECTED POEMS

About her poetry...

[This] is a book that is utterly without precedent in the poetry of this country. It has its roots in the poetry of Latin America, yet is violently and vividly the work of a poet in the United States. The language makes it so, the language not exactly as spoken, yet with the stabbing rhythms of passionate discourse among us. The book must be read as the measure of a new and daring sensibility arisen in the midst of our culture, already multifaceted and immense, yet this voice can be heard strong and true.
David Ignatow, Poet

"[These poems]...capture the beauty and violence of passion... At her best in these poems, Lynne Alvarez is a storyteller of remarkable skill...."
The Village Voice

PART I: POEMS FROM NAUTLA

Nautla is a small village on the Gulf coast of Mexico.

DOWN THE RIVER NAUTLA

"En un barquito de vela
voga, voga por el mar,
Nautla de mis amores,
Tendré que llegar,
Tendré que llegar."

Through the high sharp grasses,
Ivancito invites me to swim.
He is thin and tough
as the current.
I am white and thin,
rootless as a branch in the water.
***

A child, draped in the shadow
of a square-leafed crown of palms,
watches our boat pass.
As she has seen many boats,
she barely pauses,
a leaflet smile.
She holds her sister
in a cotton cloth
rolled in her lap.
Her eyes as liquid as the water.
***

Cresting the palmar
along the pale beach,
its fringe of palms is black,
and shakes
like a head of hair
ridding itself of the wind.
***

We are approaching the mouth
to the sea.
Waves break inward and the river
swallows salt and becomes green.

The river spreads like sugar
into the sea.

THE WOMAN WITH BLUE EYES

The woman with blue eyes
was once very beautiful,
but she comes to the house
now looking for day work
with her boy, blind in one eye
and afraid of the air—especially the wind.

She finds the moonlight wounding,
hollowing her out with its constant
wash of romance.
She stays out of the sun
to protect her skin.

Cinnamon.

And as she brings pails of
water from the well to the
sink—full of fresh
lemons to make it smell clean—
she curses the men
and blesses the boy,
screams at the boy,
and through her long blue,
blue eyes, the whites yellowed now,
through her long blue eyes,
she sees the world bluer
and meaner and crueler.

> Tia Meche closes the rectory door in a way
> so as not to awaken God and goes home.
> She sits on the second floor—rocking and
>   sewing bridal dresses.
> Her furniture is raised past last year's water mark
> waiting for this year's flood, trusting in
> God who is sleeping,
> the river,
> and snoring,
> the sea.

The woman with blue eyes
brings more and more water to the sink,

lifts the basket of tortillas and
reheats them four at a time
over the burner,
singeing them as she turns
them,
burning her fingers.

Her hair is still black
but thin.
Her eyes are ruined.
This woman wears dirty
clothes and steals and swears.
She was plucked from her bed
by men, her realm the bed and bedroom,
and now she is brought in by women,
her stall, the kitchen and yard.

The well is dark and round, gurgling
like an old man's mouth.

>   Octavio plunges into his woman
>   again and again
>   sweating and straining, slippery.
>   The windows are shuttered.
>   The hotel lies on the edge of the street.
>   The children listen at the shuttered
>   window and giggle and grunt.

The woman with the blue eyes
catches pneumonia
and her lady gives her medicine
and fires her.
Her skin is leathery
like a suitcase
so she moves on, her son
barely speaking, trembling
at the air, so much air.

She would have less air
and travels at dusk
when the world is blue,
sifting off into an horizon
which is black.

LA ÑAPA IN CHURCH

Santa Barbara,
I have laid apples at your feet,
water sparkling in the purple of their clefts;
morning and evening
I have lit candles of pink and scented wax,
that you,
exiled from the blessed company of saints,
may know I number still among your faithful.

At night I climb spires of shadow
to ignite the mouths of priests and saints
with the ruby points of my breasts.
They breathe hard and fast my sister,
in the darkness,
and their hands are wet and quick.

"Listen," I whisper in their mouths
in the darkness,
and I move my hips,
heavy with the seeds of a thousand men,
until their coins fall
clattering to my feet.

    "Cascabel"   *"Cascabel"*

(La Ñapa, literally "a little extra", here refers to a local prostitute.)

THE RIVER AND THE BRIDGE

Miguel and I walk down the road
the back of our hands
touching, electric;
the road dusty and alight
with our faces.

*("Ahhhh", the river whispers with its
silver tongue sliding the fish from the riverbed.)*

How would it be
to live with this nineteen year old
whose "good job" would give us
one room of painted brick
and a brand new stove?

*("Ahhhh", the voice of the river is strange and cool,
dark with leaves and the wet eyes of fish.)*

I see myself
a small wife
in a loose dress
standing in a hut of palm
and *chamalote*
my feet wet with dew;

the wild land rolls about me;
volcanoes worn to pulpy soil and bush.

And he would grow lean
and gritty in his work
his shirts black with oil
his hands rough and burned
My nights' salty comfort.

*("Ahhhh", the river says, its breath the scent
of wet leaves and fish
and far away and faint
of the sea.)*

We lean over the bridge
and stare out across the glistening
back of the river
riding it with our eyes

until it explodes in a brief
flash of silver
into the horizon.

*("Ahhhhhhhh", the river courses by
silent, insistent as blood between us,
smelling of ash and mold
and of fish
who pass and pass
and never touch.)*

PIPO GETS WELL

In a world so new
that many things had not
yet been named,
Pipo, the smallest,
almost died of delicacy,
every flutter of light
a heartbeat.
Once, Pipo awoke delirious
and cried,
"Mama, why am I
so much darker
than the rest?"
"Ah," his mother signed,
"I did not wash you
in a *burra*'s milk
so you did not lighten
like the others."
And Pipo awoke again
and pointed to things
asking, "What's this,
what's this?" until
the world had a name
for all things
even the smallest
and the darkest.

THE MARICA

The Marica sways his hips like a woman
and takes the boys to the beach at midnight
for a long tender kiss which they never
forget.
The Marica teaches the men to pluck and fry
their neighbor's chickens
in the early morning to eat with their rum
and brandy
they joke with him by dancing like young girls
with high voices and pinch his cheek.
The Marica dreams at night
in the blue light of the stars
he is a woman with solid arms and large breasts
and that he gives birth to the village,
sweating and spreading his thighs
until it emerges
wound in a silken cord as silver as the river.

CHILD OF PARADISE

The ball stopped in mid-air,
white against a sky,
undiluted,
so blue your eyes tear
with the immensity of its
precision.

The girls' volleyball game
was broken by Toto,
the town magistrate
come to get his bride
of the slender arms,
of the small clean feet,
her orange dress,
white teeth.
Her eyes laughed like
the amber eyes of a child,
freshly drawn against the sky.

She turned and smiled
(she turned and smiled
she turned and smiled)
as if this were a moment
of her completion, and
she could go no farther
than this moment,
than this square
half green with shadow
half white with sun.

From the park's tiny stage,
a painted Juarez and Zapata
brood flat and weary,
clinging to the peeling walls.
The country's Fathers
of scenes so familiar
they blossom into night's pageantry,
the songs of teenage boys,
the *danzón* of wide-hipped dancers
two-stepping to a wheezy combo.

And in this paradise,
walls and clothing are visitations
of a darkening age.
Toto's bride has a child each year
for five years;
two live, one dies,
one lingers and one is born
like a small blue weight
shed and buried in the shade.

She stoops and bends and curves
until she is bent and thin,
a sliver of the moon's blind arc.
Her eyes always amber,
her smile that destiny of smiles
beyond circumstance,
she lives old
from her twenty second year.

OLIVIA OLIVIA

Olivia's womb burns with another child
she blisters and swells
with this unconscious fertility
her skin is grainy, incandescent,
salt or sand glazed by the moonlight
of Maracaibo*
she shifts and shifts
tossing the covers
she cannot tolerate any binding
bruises her,
delicate as a plum
bursting with its wooden seed

when she sleeps
she dreams the river swarms with sharks
that swim up from the salt lip of the sea
where she kneels
to rub her plates with sand

and in her dreams
she calls out to her children
but her throat rasps with the silence
of a fish drowning in air

the air is green toxic,
leaves pour from the spigots
crabs flood out of the drains
spikey and blue
in a tumultuous household
her husband cannot keep his hands
from her
her smouldering flesh disturbs his sleep
diving into her wetness
she becomes seawater and he is parched
wood
he despairs
she becomes the leaking salt-caked boat he
can never caulk enough
a *flamboyan* blooms organdy and purple
at her door
*(Here Maracaibo was the name of a small beach near Nautla.)

DESERTED HOTEL AT MARACAIBO

Walking, it is dark
there is sand, and stones
and brush.
The moon has disappeared
dissolved like a ball of salt
into the sea
spreading its damp green aroma

and there are stars.

The hotel at Maracaibo rises
husky white,
its lavender windows
thick with screens mended
many times,
each passage leads
to a darker turn
away from any memory
of guests.

Yet we cross the courtyard
and Chan yells "Ho", and
we answer, "Ho",
and he stands unsteadily
with his lantern barely lit,
the thin flame
a hairline crack in the dark.

This darkness,
the heavy spirit
of the moon's blind side;
the extinguished years
of a man and a girl;
Chan's face burned black
by so many, many suns
whose light has ceased
to illumine
even in recollection.
We are penetrated by darkness
like porous ancient stone.

We hold our meager lights aloft
and climb the splintering stairs,
two icy buckets of water
from the well in hand
to wash,
groping for the right door,
and two fresh cots
an empty jar on a box
where, melting a candle's edge
with a match,
it flows and stays erect
on its own hot wax.

and the room is clean,
closed, peeling;

the screen lets nothing pass,
animal nor air,
and kneeling on the cot,
we see the beach
glistening white and
shattered by the sea,

and the nascent moon,
a far abandoned thing,
rocks,
rocks and cries
on its broken rim.

NELLI DYEING HER FLOOR

Her dress tucked up about her knees,
the lifted veil on the common flesh,
showing he soft intimacy of her thighs
become practical in her task.

She turns the chairs upside down
on the kitchen table, lifts
the mosquito netting over the beds,
raises the curtains that separate
room from room.
She rumbles among this destiny
of things inert, impatient
with their bondage
and her mastery over them.

About her,
the swamp encroaches in a soft
cascade of grasses and mud.
The throaty crescendo of beetles
and frogs roots in the steam air.

On this first of the month,
her small tide of dye washes
over the floor.*
Moving it with a rag on the end
of a pole, Nelli covers every inch,
rings out the rag, soaks it in
the dye pail, spreads it on the floor
and pushes it back and forth
as if under this careful stain
the crimson stone would bloom
warm and tireless as the earth.

The floor is dark, as glistening
as the fragile crease of her eyelids,
her smooth breasts under cotton,
the rounded freckled face
that won her a husband at fourteen,
her tiny polished nails.

*(The stone floors were dyed monthly with a red vegetable dye.)

The nets swing down, the curtains fall,
the plastic woven chairs replaced,
the table clean.
Nelli sits on a stoney ledge in her
yard, a dais of order,
her soles and fingers red,
waiting for her husband's return.

Her wide freckled face reddens
when you mention his name.

NYIN AND NAUYAQUE*

Nyin, the hunter of lizards,
lies on the planks of his boat.
The worn grey boards swell about him
like a gourd
or the welcoming arms of the weary Virgin,
her face alight with a smile so white
and pure
that it becomes the sky.

Nyin arches his back
against the rough planks of his boat,
the fangs of Nauyaque
still sunk in his chest
whispering their poison
to the silence of his heart.
Loops of glistening cold uncoil
into his fragile corset of ribs.

Nauyaque,
Fingerling snake of the swamps,
shed into the transparency of air
by the hundred distant voices
of the wind.

The great sloping roots of the mangrove
mingle black dyes with the waters.
The light and air
grow coarse with the stench of the swamp,
the mucky penitence of a millennium
of empty shells,
the sadness of the flesh of snails and fish.

In the grey wooden curve of his boat,
Nyin bends like an arc to the light,
frail as ricepaper,
spiraling through the dark watery cathedral
of swamp
to the sea.

*(Nauyaque is a small highly poisonous snake.)

PLANERIDE HOME

Leaving the far country behind,
Letting it sink into the sea
While the great continents come
Unmoored as they pass my window
Stirring the ocean into flowers of
Foam and widening their arms into
Peninsulas; I leave forever,
Foundering on the tusks of
A thousand green volcanoes; memories
Streaming from me like rain;
The bells of churches
Echoing in my throat.
I am scattered.
Blown north, south
Into mystery like the unglimpsed
Peak of Orizaba mist-hung
In July. O Eight-Year Guardian
You have betrayed me into carrying you
Away with me; Wedge against my rib, are
You sword or are you shield?

GRACIELA'S STORY

I

Those palms, black and solitary along the sea,
were outposts of an horizon that simply measured
from here to there.
Now the distances have grown so vast
the faintest echo of the greatest cry
is lost,

and men I knew have wandered off alone
into their separate deaths.

I still return here fitfully each year
touching this familiar splintered porch
and walking barefoot to the pastures, blue
and steaming with dew,
as I did every morning of my childhood.

II

Swarming down the road like a lost army,
You can almost hear the slap of their barefeet.
The men and boys first.
The women trailing behind holding up slaughtered
pigs and hens.
Blood and water at their feet.

The *campesinos* are coming to honor my brother this year,
and that is only as it should be.
Without him they would be wading through mud
every spring when the river rises,
and boiling their milk every night
to keep it from curdling.
How I like to see them this way.
The men with the points of their machetes
glittering in the sun,
and the boys,

eager as the dogs nipping their heels.
Hah! In any corner of the world
I could tell a ranchero from Carranza
by the cock of his hat.
The men of Vega de A La Torre three miles away
wear their hats on the back of their heads
like farm boys,
but these are truly men.

They say this is the finest land in the Republic.
Vanilla grows here and mango, banana.
The Brahma cattle we fatten on our land
are imported from Brazil,
a special breed from the tropics,
white and heavy in the mists.

To the north, along the fringe of palms, is Nautla
where the river meets the sea.
Its streets are smooth and green with grass.
You can ride there on horseback in three hours.
I have done it many times.

Everything grows here.
Spit out an orange seed and you will have a tree.

This land wasn't always ours.
Those fields behind our house to the east
belonged to Don Felix and his ten sons,
the *caciques*—the strongmen of this place.
Who would not be strong with ten sons?
With ten sons, taking one life
would be like opening a dam for the rest of us
to pour through.

In two generations sixty men were killed,
a priest was blinded and a young girl split
and mated with a mule.
Don Felix and his sons would return,
their skins pallid with dust,
But he has been dead thirty years now.
He died when I was newly fifteen—
lying on the floor of his jeep with half his face
blown away,
And the small silhouette of an Indian from Carranza
racing his horse into the thin curve of the moon.

I remember, one night my brother came for me at school
in the mountains of Puebla.

Four hundred years it has stood there
chisled from the icy slopes of Iztlacihuatl.
My fingers were cold as I came down the stairs
feeling for the wall with one hand.
There were no lights,
not even a candle lit on the stairwell.
I plunged into a subterranean river
that only surfaces in caves.

My brother Arturo stood in the light of the courtyard
with a gun in his belt and his arms crossed
on his chest,
his shadow flickered like a moth
against the wall.

In Carranza, guns are as common as chickens or plows.
My father, when he was alive, used to fold
the cartridge belt carefully every night
and put his gun high on the kitchen shelf.
For my baby sister, Blanca, Banquita,
was killed by a shot from that gun—
such a tiny coffin—she was less than a year.
My father's gun slipped from the holster hung on
the chair and discharged.
The bullet passed through my mother's forefinger
and thumb, and burst the eye of my sister
at her breast.
That is why there are only two of us—where families
are big—ten, thirteen.
My mother forgave my father many things,
but she would have no more children.

That night in October, we headed south to the coast.
It was dark but I could smell the sweetness
of the green along the road.
I knew the way,
Unseen the cliffs, the jungle flowers and vines
pouring like a waterfall from the sides of the mountains,
the mossy pyramids.

It was almost dawn when we arrived home.
The edges of the sky were fading to grey as if
they were already old,
and the dogs howled in the wind
with almost human voices.
We walked from the bus down the road.
The grass was wet with dew, though the sky

was dry and empty.
The house was a hole in the night,
and my father's red mare, black in the night,
stood by the door.
There was no noise and only a small light,
a single candle shone like an eye from the house.
Finally I saw the moon low over the palms
near the river,
and felt the cool silver of its crescent smile
and was afraid.

My mother sat like a stone
in her chair, rocking on the dark porch,
and my brother, Arturo, knelt at her side.
But I stood back and stared into each blind hole
in the wooden posts that supported the roof.
There were holes in the plaster walls and the bricks,
so many of them, they looked like
droplets of spattered paint.
Inside, we walked on a carpet of splinters.

I never saw my father again.
We buried him in a box of *mangle* and bronze,
and at night, I would hear my brother plead with my mother
and rage: "Who did it? *Hijos de su madre*! I want their
names so I can match their blood with his. Let me use
it in the fields to fertilize the grass.
I would slit their throats and use their very teeth
to plow the land."
My mother would never answer.

A month before I was fifteen, Don Felix
came to the house:
Don Felix, the strongman, the *cacique* with ten
fullgrown sons;
Don Felix who drove a jeep and always came
with twelve men on horses at his back.

He was a big man with a barrel chest and a mustache
red with tobacco.
His father was a colonel during the Revolution -
that is why his family kept so much land,
which should have belonged to us
and to the *ejidos** of the Indians near Carranza.

*(Ejidos are communal Indian lands.)

This Colonel kept his private army after the war
and gave his men land and the women on it.
And when they had drunk their credit at his cantinas,
he took their land and gave them back their pistols
and machetes for his private wars in Nautla, in
Hicaltepec of the backwaters and pitched roofs, in Vega.

Two nights after our return,
my brother raised his rifle to the dry sound
of gravel under Don Felix's jeep.
He fired two shots in the air over his head,
and my mother, who never held a gun in her life,
held up the pistol that killed Blanquita.
Don Felix's men rumbled close to the jeep.
Their faces that mixture of arrogance and fear
I have seen so often on the faces
of the *pistoleros* who serve our politicians.

Don Felix turned to look at me, for I was the first
to venture out of the house
after my brother.
In those days, indeed, I was pretty.
Slim and blond, quick as a fish.
You can ask anyone and they will say so.
And I knew,
because he came at ease and smiled at us
as if it were spring
and my father were alive,
and because my mother had reached for the gun
when she heard his jeep,
I knew that he had killed my father.

"Doa Espinoza" called Don Felix, "I am truly sorry
for the violence that killed your husband,
but remember we are neighbors, and I am strong."
He gestured toward his land and then to the twelve men
behind him.
The meaning lay with his men.

My mother stood still, her face white, black dress drifting
against the graying sky and the rough mud of the yard,
the darkening hills stretching north toward Nautla.
She said nothing and Don Felix turned his jeep sharply
and left.
His men jerked their horses around,
passing so close that their tails
brushed our faces.

We did not move.

The next day, I took my father's pistol off
the kitchen shelf
and carried it to Arturo, who was mending
the water pump in our shed.
"Arturo, I want to learn to use this gun," I said.

It was October and the north winds were blowing.
Arturo said the wind must die down and then
we would go to the fields and practice
with pieces of wood and live ducks,
but that was not soon enough.

Ramon Huesca was working with my brother
on the pump.
They were both slick with grease to the elbow.
Ramon was a neighbor, married
 with three girls and eyes as hot and grey as live ash.
When he was there, I would
walk back and forth in the patio feeling his heat
from the barn.
I watched his hands now,
as he held the oiled pieces of the pump,
ready to give them to my brother, one by one.
He knew I was watching.
My brother and Ramon took out rags
and soaked them in kerosene
to rub off the grease.
Then they soaped their arms and rinsed them
in an old feed trough.
My brother left to place the pump in the well
near the village and Ramon looked at me:
"*Guera**, you were staring at me" he smiled.
"What do you see that is so strange?"
"You are not strange at all" I replied.
He moved closer to me and I did not move away.
"*Guera*," he said touching my forehead, my hair,
"I can teach you to shoot the gun.
I can teach you near the cattle pens in the village
where the school stops the wind."

I looked at him and watched him smile.
His white teeth flashing with chips of gold.

*(*Guera* is a Mexican term that refers to a light-skinned, light-haired person.)

And he took off the buttons from my blouse with his knife,
but gently,
and my blouse sprung open like a new leaf,
and he touched my breasts and kissed the nipples
and I held his head.
He slid me under him and I thought,
"Ah, this is what it is", and I loved him
then because he was warm and knew me,
and I would not go as a virgin
to kill this man who killed my father.

III

When I turned fifteen, I rode to Nautla on my father's
mare to buy some cloth.

I dressed like a man that day
because the north winds were still blowing
in from the coast, and it was a cold ride of three hours.
I loved Nautla.
It was full of light-haired Spaniards then
and ships that came upstream to load before
going out to sea.
The streets were filled with grass.
There were no cars and few wagons;
most of the traffic took a road that passed
on one side of the town to reach the barges
that ferried them across the river.
Nautla was peaceful and clean.
Even when it rained
the houses were free of mud and you could walk
barefoot in the streets, and the people turned
like sunflowers to your face.

They said I looked like an Indian from Carranza that day
and laughed at my baggy pants and my hair,
tangled because I tucked it up under a sombrero
which I cocked over my eye
as we all do in Carranza to this day.
I carried my father's pistol with me,
wrapped in a kerchief and tied around my neck
inside my shirt, like a heavy pendant.
I could feel it thumping on my chest as I rode,
A second fearful heart.

In daylight, you could not mistake I was a woman,
but at dusk,
when I started back to our ranch,
I was only a small dark figure—from Carranza
by the cock of my hat.

And riding home that night,
I passed Don Felix in his jeep.
I was close and he recognized me
and he called out, "*Adiós* Graciela."
and I answered him, as was polite,
"*Adiós*, Don Felix".
And he called out, his voice
carrying in the wind, "Graciela, Gracielita,
where are you going on a night like this,
dressed like a man?"

And I called back,
"Don Felix, you don't want to know
where I am going".

And he laughed and threw back his head,
the wind raking his hair through the open window
as he rode along beside me in his jeep,
and it was dark and bitter cold with wind.
I left the road for the fields at its side
and Don Felix turned his wheel and kept steady by me.
And he laughed and threw back his head,
the wind raking his hair through the open window
as he rode along beside me in his jeep,
and it was dark and bitter cold with wind.
I left the road for the fields at its side
and Don Felix turned his wheel and kept steady by me.

"Gracielita, come take a ride with me,"
he called smiling into the wind.

And I answered, "Don Felix, you don't want me
to take a ride with you".

He sped up, turning a bit in front of me,
so I had to turn my mare too,
heading toward the hills with the wind in my ears
and his voice at my side.

"Graciela, you are beautiful.
Come sit beside me where it is warm.
I will keep you dry."

His words echo even now,
and I see the ground roll black under my horse's hooves.
And when we reached the base of the hill
I stopped my father's mare and dismounted.
Don Felix stopped his jeep and opened the door.

I remember,
shifting through the smells of the men I have had since then,
I remember,
he smelled of Spanish cognac and smoke, and
he was warm when he kissed me.
He laughed softly as he pulled out the gun
wrapped and hanging close to my chest.
He took my hands and kissed them on the palms.
Father, I remembered your mare,
sweating in the north wind
standing riderless next to the jeep,
and I shot Don Felix as he unfastened his belt,
and I rode my mare slowly down the hill and
left him.

IV

The next year, I went to school.
I married Moises, my first husband, when I was seventeen.
He was a lieutenant in the army, and we moved
north near Monterrey.
It was too hot there and dry.

Arturo stayed.
He built the new cattle pens with sprays
for the *ejidos*;
He gave money for a school for the villagers;
and he picked off thirty-nine men,
one by one,
of those who rode with Don Felix
the night they pulled my father from the house—
while my mother hid trembling in the patio—
and hung him dying in the pasture,
turning in the wind.

PART II: CEREMONIES OF EARTH

DOG AND HERMIT CRAB

Dog he be romping on the beach
sand in the crack of his paw
waves thumping.
Dog he be romping on the beach
And Hermit Crab come
scuttling and stopping
scuttling and stopping
in his borrowed shell
little legs pumping, little legs
scraping spiney trail in the sand.
Dog stops and sniffs.
Hermit he disappears.
"Who are you?", Dog sniffs,
"What you be?" sniff.
"Go away wet nose,
your tongue's too hot to be ocean
your breath's too stale to be air.
Go away
You be in my light",
says Hermit Crab.
Dog raise his tail and wag.
He wait for Hermit Crab panting.
The sea be coming in
closer and closer.
Hermit Crab he see this
and he grab his shell and run.
He scamper right into that sea.
"Ha, ha", he says. "Ha, ha,
I got the whole damn ocean now!"
All Dog can do is bark.
He bark happy too,
raising sand.
He happy and say,
"O K Crab, O K. You just wait.
I got the whole damn beach!"

LIVING WITH NUMBERS

<u>NUMBERS</u>

When God opened His great fist
and spilled the stars into the sky,
He laughed.
He laughed and in His pleasure
even He lost count.

<u>NUMBERED</u>

ONE bears witness
disguised as the enemy
among us,
the burning stake
the bloody pike is his,
the mother covering her
child's eyes.
One watches and remembers.
One is the tower and the well,
the woman rocking in the street.
One is the empty house, the empty pocket,
the glass about to be filled.

TWO is always hungry,
the double-barreled shotgun
propped against his chin,
the knock on the door,
the stillness of night.
Two is the black horse and rider,
the streak of horizon.
Nose to nose and belly to belly,
two is always hungry
and in mortal danger.

***

THREE is a child.
FOUR is hardly stable,
the table wobbles
the window warps from its frame.
FIVE has seen it all
and doesn't give a damn anymore.

Five flicks up the shade
and drinks his wine in public.
       ***

SIX smokes in the dark
on the porch,
the spangled river sings
below like tambourines.
Six takes a young wife
and hides from death.
Six is the speckled moon,
the circling owl's shadow
on the hare.
       ***

SEVEN is the silken priest
cool blessings slip from his
fingers like jewels
onto the bent heads of the poor.
EIGHT are the posts along the road,
the steps of stone.
NINE is death or the prism,
the child old before her time,
the cross and the light,
the last friend, the
midnight call.
TEN is the wheel of fire
ten is the wheel spinning.
My heart is the wheel
and I am the brown-haired
girl wading
in the lake.
The red sun rises.
The dying moon fades.
Tiny crayfish scuttle
in the shade.
I see the purple storm clouds banking,
the old man yawning,
the corn leaves crackling
in the field.
My hair is sky
My eyes long willow leaves
The young girl becomes
everything she sees.

Quick now
They way to heaven is through a closing door.

END OF THE WORLD

The fire engines came
and smoke and noise and flames
and people running
and the little girl with dark
eyes and a mouth smeared
with dirt cried and said
"Es el fin del mundo"
"What?" they asked me.
"It's the end of the world",
I said.

THE MAN WITH TEARS

There is a plump man
in a rumpled green suit
coming towards me.
Tears roll and roll down his cheeks.
He is sobbing.
Surely he has lost a child,
the most terrible death;
or his mother,
and the child in himself
has died

The world is old
old and men cry
and children die.

DARK SINAI

An hortatory prayer for Yom Kippur

A pillar of smoke, You appeared to us
In the desert, smouldering before the
Idols, brooding over our enemies and
Dark in the face of our people.

Thunder on the mountain and fire on stone
You came down to us, flaming from the hands
Of Moses and fierce in the words of our
Prophets, deadly in the wars of our dispersal.

The Law was our light, You said, shining
In our eyes like an open furnace, and It
Shall guide us to the Land of Israel, the
Promise and the Covenant, for we
Are the Chosen People.

And the bare steppes of Sinai flowered
At these words in the Torah. Words as You
Gave us words, history, song, penance
Love. We poured them out and soaked them
In as hungrily as water poured on the coarse
Sands of the desert. Words that curdled the
Blood of our enemies who brought down their
Axes in disgust. We were a Holy People.
But it was not enough.
We passed and were passed.

And You cast again the black shadow of
Sinai long upon the continents, the pillar
Of smoke returned, Thunder and fire on
Stone and the world was an open furnace
Soaking our blood like the hungry porous
Sand of the desert.

Remember now,
That it may never happen again.

It was not enough.

No gravestone stands at Babi Yar, the
Earth no longer puckers and smokes with
The gases of the buried dead. Auschwitz,
Treblinka, Dachau, Buchenwald, Riga are
Blank and cold

But know these names
As you know the names of your children
For it was not enough.
It was not enough
That children dreamed green meddler trees
And cities they would never see
Again; at three and four they closed their
Mouths to drugs, fed to quiet them
Saying "no", they knew and would be quiet
With no need of them; and families holding
Hand to hand, pointed upward to God
Grey on a leaden horizon beyond the pits
Of their graves; and those to die lay down
Naked on the dying heaps, stroking those
Beneath to comfort them.

This was not enough.

For when the nations exhumed the massive
Weight of bodies and the shrill, rusty screams
Of the holocaust, of the dead:
"We did not open our doors, the doors were closed
And we did not see", They said.

And so, we are the stone and the fire
Streaming down the mountain
Where this multitude was opened into death.
Bones white, blood red
But we are vaster now, as vast as the
Spirits writhing over Europe in the curling
Smoke, those that perished and those that
Smote, as vast as the parameters of the
Good and evil we understand.

For this remember,
That it was not enough.

The Law is not the thundering word or
Stricken tablet. It is cast in this shadow
And yet hangs trembling on the gibbet.
For these are the final measures of our Law:
Our sovereign will and our immortal spirit.

THE CALM OF AUGUST WITH THE FURIES IN HOT PURSUIT

Pushed down the gas pedal
to the floor
ffffffffffffffftttttttt!
the lights whizz by
so fast they become one
orange ball bounces
on the edge of the highway
and rolls off
sunset
indeed
still
the radio turned up so high
shrapnel music blasts my
bones to smithereens
a thousand dreams
my heart jumps
jumbled in its own
wet web of physicality
pinned down, hemmed in, squirming
ffffffffffffffftttttttt!
I want the light to hurt my eyes
till I go blind
I want the sound to burst my ears
Pulverized
I want to leave it all
behind.

CROSSROADS IN THE HEARTLAND

The long silver diesels
with gaseous bowels
trundling along the highways,
four gas-stationed corners
rising out of nowhere,
crossroads,
the sudden choice flickering
dark green in summer wheat,
telephone lines,
billboard signs
and the double edged two-way road
stretches on forever.
Do I stop here?
Can I read the glyphs of mountain spines
and riverbeds?
Uprooted how do I plant myself
get dirt beneath my nails
the proof of grabbing hold
and digging in? I got roots see...
This is the heartland.
This is nowhere.
Am I the haunted owl in the woods
or only the rabbit's skipping foot?

No se que tienen las flores
las flores del camposanto
cuando las mueve el viento
parecen que estan llorando.

The dead can't stay
packed in, stacked up, stowed together.
They must rise to heaven.
There's no rest below
you know
what with roots sliding and hissing
like blind cold snakes and buried
lightening ricocheting though
the lost chambers of the earth,
startling the dead so they rise and hover
like vapor,
their eyes and mouths round in an
interminable "ooooohhhh" of surprise .
They rise so quickly
before their bodies turn to stone
and race toward the fiery-maned sun,
the roaring sun.
So it is you, my friends, who circle
my head like vaporous "Os" of wonder
and bewilderment
finding us so divided after
such intimacy
as distinct as water and horizon
as sun and silhouette
an illusory proximity where we cleave
but never touch.
Go on ahead then, my friends,
go on, rise, ride a polished stallion
a dragon with amethyst eyes,
rise, eat salt, the great preserver,
and scatter mist and light,
leave a trail so I can follow.

NEW YORK CITY: The Hudson River

So this is the mighty Hudson brought to its knees
The majestic flow of water turned to poison
not by the hot blood of war,
the stockpiling of idealism into the
stoney blue corpses of the young,
not by the haunting mold of the
Church or pitiless starvation
or monsoons covering green moons
and silken skies.

So this is the Hudson gushing the living
and the dead,
the surface glitters with life, the sun kneels
and hangs diamond chokers on the water in
daytime elegance not seen since the monarchy,
the banks statuesque and subtle—
here towers and spires—the solid hand of
man
here the rainbow's arc of God,
But it has turned to poison, the long cold poison
of indifference, a hatred so profound
that we will rot away with it,
gouging parts of ourselves until we are revealed,
scaly, remorseless, hopeless as lepers....

FRIDAY NIGHT AND A YOUNG LADY GOES OUT WITH HER LOVER

Flowered silk
tottering heels
silver stars dangle
happily from her ears
the wind blows fragrance and warmth
over the silver lake
the girl gleams
believing his every word
which grows truer
and truer every time he looks at
her
the hem of her dress flutters
with delicacy
and if we could look we'd still
find traces of talcum and rose cream
between her breasts

The sea roars and swells
above me
my lone heart leaps
that dolphin part of me

THE DREAMING MAN

In a white room
as white as parchment
or sailcloth
the shades are drawn
like eyelids with that faint
flutter of wind against
greenshadowed corners,
creases of green shadow.
There lies the dreaming man
on a thin metal bed, pale,
wind fluttering in his chest,
chasing whispers and liquids
through his veins.
It is the dreaming man.

"He's always like this",
the nurse bows to the doctor.
"Not a word is true",
nods the doctor.
They step on fallen steel pins
as they leave.

And the dreaming man, dreaming,
dreaming his sons were dying.
the last one's breath on his cheek,
two days beard and fever made him
childishly soft.
The earth shifted.

His cornfields were ripped apart,
the wheat split down the middle
as if a jagged hacksaw cut
bits away.
Then his wife grew old and turned
to dust.
She blew into his eyes
and made him weep.
The animals moaned in the field.

The nurse laughs,
"No, no. He's from the city".

"He never married",
the doctor confirms.
Plastic pens break under their shoes as they leave.

Now his dreams tangle and arch like mangrove roots
mired in water blue-black as kohl,
secret as the Nile-eyes of women.
He dreams of women's legs encased in soft
leather boots and men's calves wrapped around them
naked and bronze with dark hairs clinging to the flesh.
They laugh together softly, happily.
young children rush up in uniforms
in greys and plaid with white collars
bringing the little cheerful news of the streets.
He dreams of statues of eagles
and horses as large as whole mountains in sunlight.

He dreams of the greenest mosses
enfolding stone and creeping into the heat
over the tombs of Indian kings in Palenque
and Chichen Itzà.
He dreams the glittering ocean and its salt desert shore in southern Spain.
He dreamed the cropped cranberry bogs dyeing
their waters red,
reflecting in the quietness of red waters the grey
silken skies of autumn.
He dreams until his soul breaks through
his body like the wick through a candle.

In the white room with white
walls and green shadows, the nurse
points,
"See how he is curling up
like a dried leaf?"
The doctor kisses her mouth to quiet her.
"He is consuming himself", he says.

Like the wick through wax
His soul works through his body.
He makes love and trembles in his sleep
like the wick through a flame.

AN ANGEL IS SINGING OUTSIDE MY WINDOW

I hear an angel singing
outside my window.
He is keening
like a long silver wire
in the wind.
He has tears on his cheeks
and his heart is red.
He is hovering there
streaming rainbows so
he can see
all things in all ways.

It takes the imperfect
to be seen,
so he is obviously
an imperfect angel.
His skin is diaphanous
and his robes translucent,
a mere rustle
sounds not substance,
so he is singing.

Dogs wail.
Birds pierce his wrists
and circle his waist.
We all lean out of our windows,
blotted by raindrops and the small
particles of soot within raindrops.

We can barely see him,
a great clashing voice
out there
in the wind and the lightening.

There is an angel singing outside my window.

CEREMONIES OF EARTH

Your body betrays your speeding thoughts
(Fine-spun as sunlight streaked with dust)
It moves with the ceremonies of earth
The heavy baptism of gravity pulling it steadily
Toward the final mute benediction of dirt
And stone.

Amazement rounds your eyes
Glistening in quick echo to
Your flesh and the kindling of sex
Hot and moist on a bed where you
Pass from one generation to another.

This eludes you (Is this mortality?)
And you turn to me
Stroking my skin as if I were the earth
Fertile with welcome for
Your return.

JOHN McCULLOUGH TALKS TO REPORTERS IN THE MOONLIGHT

"I jus like to see 'em fall, slow
like in the movies
drops of blood spread
sailing through the air
as if they don' belong nowhere
and land, spla-a-a-t like rain
on a river."

Said John McCullough.
The moon rolled like a silver bearing
down a shaft into his chest.

"No, I don' feel too bad when I shoot
a man, cuz
I figure any man wants to get killed
rather'n give up his money,
should be dead."

SATURN MOON

In the world of spheres
Saturn and your moon conjunct
Trailing though space;
The sailboat and its keel
plunging through
a darkening lake.

LUCIFER FALLING

With his great wings afire
and the skin boiling from his back
he rushed toward the earth
and plunged his arms, his nostrils
the bones cracked to the marrow
into the damp black soil
and from the root tips he whispers
darkness   darkness

THE MAN WHO WAS LOVED BY PIGEONS

The man who was loved by pigeons
                                  sat in the park,
Looped in his grey knitted cap and rusty scarf
Though it was far too warm and
                              only his face
Showed simple and white as a stone
In the sun.
        And the pigeons landed
                              and settled
Proletariat doves, straddling the toes of his shoes
With their rustling message of peace,
                                and they graced
The old man
With the care they reserved for fountains and the steep
Buttresses
      of churches.

The man loved by pigeons sat with a red paper bag
Stuffed to the brim
                      with white popcorn
Yellow-tinged,
          And the birds shuffled closer, their
Horny beaks dipped
And tore at its side till
                    it gave,
And their grey fluted wings and crusty feet brushed
His ankles and thighs as they ate.
This was their love, then, their glutted desire, and they
                                babbled and chirped.

        "*I am ruined,*" he said softly
Speaking of love, while
The pigeons warbled, "Ruined, ruined cluck
Chirp",
        Twisting their necks to these choicest
Of words.

             The ruined man who was loved by pigeons sits
                                        in the dark
Alone on his bench where the pigeons still flock
Though the popcorn is gone
The bag stripped
               and torn
                            And they mill at his feet
With low trills of compliance until
                              the thin edge of the wind
Peels them back from the square
                      like an old grey skin.

THE GIRL WHO SAW RAINBOWS

Old wives tales and whispers guard the coming spring.
A miscast shadow, rumor, a shaft of light and the rainbow's
Misty prow has come to rest again on these vespers
Of the changing seasons.
Charcoal clouds and sulfur skies stretch beyond—
The faint margins of a biblical hell still imprinted on
The evening.
The faulty skein of the sky and road
Has strung me out from place
To place,
Sprung me like the rainbow from
A leaden eye,
Only to disappear into the morning.

Paper lanterns on a string, the colors of
The rainbow, arch madly
Giddy in the wind.
What has it come to?

A collage of sex, one face upon another.
Those first daring, perverted games with urine and feet
And unformed breasts, touching hidden parts
In hidden fields,
The grey sky bellowing above us like a lost rutting cow
In the sudden storm.

(I turn to you now, turn and see myself still turning
in the red room of a New York hotel, red and pink
as the chambers of the heart,
vulva, penis damp, dispensed—the darkened rooms, attic
floors, doorways, beaches, boyfriends' cars—all filled
with the thrust of desire studded with incestuous doubt.
I turned to you now, shy with these leftover years.
My life's a question.)
Over the lumbering, virginal road ahead,
The rainbow mounts the sky
Again and again and again.

CLOWNS AND ANGELS

At times, you look at me and
My spirit wavers. Shadows
Dramatize a pose, a look of
Sudden candor. Shadows that
Stretch out like a cat beside me
In the half-light. Your voice tapers
Off behind me, a torch half flame
Half smoke and together we travel
Circles broken like the moon, mid-
Month, slivery threads, as if I
Were an etching, you an artist
With tracing fingertips, and close
Beside us, laughing behind gentle
Hands come clowns and angels,
Gladly waiting to show us all they
Know, spreading their fingers with
Laughter to let small stars escape
From their throats and soar above
Us till we take notice and dance.

WHEN YOU ARE OLD

When you are old
And mysterious to me,
A dim figure on a
Fragile horizon,
Think back
Across the years,
That on some summer
Nights we broke out
Of ugliness and
Fled,
Two conspirators
With bottles full of
Wine and joyous music
On the radio.
And remember
If
You
Can
That it was right and
Fine and sometimes
More, and we left
Pain,
That interminable fire,
Only scorching
Our heels.

THE VIRGIN

Time lapsed into a quietude
She didn't comprehend.
Years were open-ended,
Spring and fall seasons of
Tumbling winds and leaves.
Loves became friendships,
Fond and faraway like smiles
On stairways and old pictures.
Yet she walked carefully
With loose hair and fine fingers,
Always stepping to the threshold
And holding out her hand
To be taken.

GOD SAVES THE SOUL—THE INNOCENT

Her dreams were made
Of plasterboard
And paste,
Colored in haphazardly
In haste.
Exposed to all the
Elements, they never
Survived one.
Fire and air laid
Them waste,
Earth and water
Covered them.
Yet she smiled and
Built again patiently
And chaste.

He said all women were whores
and to prove it he sent
his mother lacey cards and fruits
and whispered phone calls
until she agreed to meet with him.
And when she walked through the door
pale and anxious in black
her heart full of colors
He flashed his teeth and said
"You see, all women are whores"

I LOVED BUT ONCE

I loved once but not again
Blindly and sullenly and
Completely
I loved a boy
Until he was a man,
Green-eyed, as drunk as I
Was with golden skin and
Arms that smelled of smoke
And grass and ached for
Something as liquid and
Eternal as love.
Once
But never again was I
Struck and lost like a
Wavering match
In the wind. Yet we loved
Until his name became
Commonplace and his face
Was fierce and misty with tears.
And the years crashed in
One upon another, rolling and
Breaking over other arms and
Thighs, smooth backs and buttocks,
But I only have loved
Once at best,
And pitched a tent in darkness
And bid the moon in
With the rest.

LEAVING MY DAUGHTER AT SCHOOL...
AND LOOKING FORWARD AND BACK

Soft hair and hands, the ritual glance of
A first Schoolday, a new game where the
Corridors are lit, the floors are dim and
The ancient voices of children rise
Above the din—calling out in victory from
A mountaintop—out—over the roar of
Avalanches, and under the hard white layers
Of cold gathering in silence.

They tumble about us, like Indian spirits
Suddenly freed...children of Thebes, children
Of Antioch, ancient and invisible - back, back
To some eternal, mad fascination with shapes
And sounds. A-a-a-a-Arabesque, apple, apple
Rrred, greeen. A benediction on our seamless
Tongue and throat wells around us and my daughter's
Good-bye stops and whirls on the head of a pin.

CHANGE OF SKIN

They fall from me
like old skin
My grandmother tears out of me
splitting me as if I were her cocoon
and now she can escape
She steps out, her long brown
wings are wet and new
She spreads them out, beating lightly
and then she spirals off into the stars
My mother pecks and pecks at me
succeeding in opening a crack
she hatches
all fluff and hunger
and scampers off leaving twig prints
mixed with dust and the soft yellow dung
of baby chicks
I peel off my skin
thin and parchment clear in the light
I walk through the streets
red and new
big hands plucking summer mangoes
and grey buildings
turning their steamy eyes
to me
I stick the green stem of a hibiscus
through my hair
and sing

Cambio de piel

She loved him all her life
and when she thought he might die
she tied her wrist to his at night
so that his pulse would not flutter
away from her suddenly
and leave her stranded

My grandmother runs howling through the house
In terrible pain
Holding her head as the spectre of death
Rushes before her in some macabre game of tag
Where she is always "IT".
We stand helpless, aghast as she approaches,
A drugged swimmer in a maelstrom.
"Now is it time? Another pill?
Why won't you help me...Please dear mother help me".
Eighty years pressing against her skull and she
Cries for her mother to ease the pain.

Oh grandmother, that I were a witch or a fury
And knew the secrets of the night,
I would take you with me flying, black on black
Across the skies,
We would travel back, with the wind tangling our hair,
Back to Nebraska where the Russian boys
Felt your breast and thigh and kept you from school
In fear.
We would let darkness cover them so you would forget
And be at peace,
but I am earthbound and helpless.
The night is a secret slashed by the moon.
And other memories vie for you attention
Like jealous children.

Mother to mother to mother—we are daughters all.
Daughter, mother, ghost, I watch you
Burn, still in the pogroms in the Ukraine
Cowering on the floor in tortured memory
Calling to your mother, "Mother, please",
To ease the pain.

SINCE THEY TOLD ME

Since they told me you were dead

I have seen your face again and again
floating with an inestimable smile
                 (your lips always soft)
and your eyes green as new leaves
turned to some light, perhaps to sunlight
through a window after we had made love.

How strange we should meet and meet
in this luminary sphere
where you continue smiling
as if having blasted apart your skull
you had forced open some long-awaited door.

I will never know if you were going out
                 or in.
Since they told me, Jimmy, you were dead

through the intermittent silence of these days
the great choir of the past joins in,

though we had grown like separate spokes
radiating from a central core.

Indeed, you are here no more.

And people run up boldly to take your
final measure
as if you would yield to tape.
     Seen from "beginning to end"
have you become so quantifiable?

I think not.

For who could ever measure the incense
of your body moving into mine?
the distance traveled beyond their farthest cry
where we remained immutable
                   irreparable?

SNOWSTORM

The last corner of the universe is
Untucked, turned inside
Out and shaken clean.
White particles fall
Endlessly from star
To space,
And flutter into place
With the deadly precision of
The eyelid of a southern belle
Bent on conquest.

* * *

The horizon is going blind,
Under rampant attack,
Struggles valiantly to maintain
Its strict line of
Order.
But the sky fills, is
Wild, passionate and indistinct
With snow, the
Horizon overcome.

* * *

All movement slows and stops, machines
Have long since reeled and sputtered
Into stillness, abandoned in snowy
Cliffs and reefs on empty, snow-
Filled streets, and now
The airy spaces—silence between
Flake and flake—
Elegant, uninhabited and
Cold, persist,
And then,
Accumulate.

MORNING TRAFFIC

The sky is white.

In this milky air, we close together
breakfast bright in pearly
capsules, liquid
somnambular
we glide forward on steamy currents
of exhaust

Sealed in glass
we chant the words of songs
to music as silent as dreams
to those outside

Inside
we are the soft meat of clams.

A man's thought glances off
the windshield
striking him so he calls out to
himself
raising his fist against an unknown
opponent
he holds his silver car
to course
one-handed
gleaming like a chariot

A
girl weeps
quietly in her stationwagon
taken with the contours
of her face shimmering with tears
in the rearview mirror
but
how the tears only care for the
purest bone and keep to the up-angle
of her cheek
or linger on the blunt line of chin

Traffic flows
and we are pulled apart by a

mammoth truck
exposing its rows of black gummy
tires
the work of a strange vivisectionist
has placed those ponderous feet
of elephants
beside us
their organic smell rises
hot and raw
through the open window

CANTO DO SERTÃO

Aaeeiioweeiii.
The bushman, the boneman comes
down from the hills, a dusty packet
of bones tied to his wrist.
His parched white flute
at his lips,
moans like the wind
through a fissure.

The bitter voices of bitter people
scatter before him, small
dry chaff that barely whispers
over stones,
while the boneman's given voice
is in the passage of things
other than himself:
the arrogant hiss of the sea
the clatter of bones.

I hear him
as in a distant canyon
picking his way through
the living to the dead,
and the marrow in my bones
sings with blood.
My rib cage springs alive.
My secret skeleton smiles
crackling with delight.

www.ingramcontent.com/pod-product-compliance
Lightning Source LLC
Chambersburg PA
CBHW061758110426
42742CB00012BB/1929